With realism, clarity, and  s
just how profoundly and pr   e
Reformation remain today.   il
if they can learn these lesso

                                                                 es
President and Professor of Theology, ⌐⌐⌐   gy

This is a fabulous recounting of the lives of five key figures of the European Reformation. It is a recounting that also reveals that if these lives had not been lived, western history and the story of the Church would be completely different. This is usable history at its best.

Michael A. G. Haykin
Professor of Church History, The Southern Baptist Theological Seminary

Lee Gatiss's *Light After Darkness* does what it says on the tin: Lee helpfully shows how the Protestant Reformers (Zwingli, Tyndale, Luther, Calvin, and Cranmer) regained, retold, and relied on the gospel of grace. Lee shows not only how these Reformers faced their own contexts of darkness but also applies the regained principles to our modern contexts; so, for example, he suggests that we should 'live in the light of the truth', just as Zwingli did in the light of his own sinfulness, rather than being tempted to shove evidence of our own depravity under the carpet 'in a mistaken belief that it might harm the truth'. Overall Lee takes us, as the Reformers did, back to God's authority as described in the Scriptures.

Andy Lines
Missionary Bishop and Chairman of the Anglican Mission in England

Have we lost our Reformation heritage? What is it that the church needs to regain today from the Protestant reformers? What are we relying on for evangelism and Christian growth? What is worth retrieving from our history by rehearsing and retelling afresh in our own worship and discipleship? By answering these crucial questions, Lee Gatiss brings gospel light to dark areas of the contemporary church. Like the Reformers, the church today needs to regain, retell, and rely on the gospel of grace.

Aimee Byrd
Author of *No Little Women* and *Why Can't We Be Friends?*

In a winsome, yet honest and penetrating examination of some of its leading characters, Lee Gatiss shows how the Reformation sheds light on some of today's vexing theological, ethical, and ecclesiastical questions. This insightful and at times provocative volume is further proof that the Reformation cannot be revisited too often, and sight of its lasting legacy must not be lost in successive generations.

Iver Martin
Principal, Edinburgh Theological Seminary

Light after Darkness provides an excellent entry point into the essence of the Reformation, and mines much of the Reformers' wisdom for our twenty-first-century context. Great biblical and practical encouragement for church leaders and members, and thus highly recommended!

Mark Earngey
Lecturer in Christian Thought, Moore Theological College, Sydney

In his usual eloquent and articulate style, Dr Lee Gatiss illuminates the wisdom of the Protestant Reformers and the continuing truth of Almighty God's gospel of grace. *Light After Darkness* compels the reader to stand firm in the foundation of faith which was courageously taught by men and women of the 16th century.

Julian Dobbs
Bishop of the Convocation of Anglicans in North America

Lee Gatiss's treatment of how the Protestant Reformers regained, retold, and relied on the gospel of grace – and what we can learn from them – in *Light After Darkness* is historically informed, accessibly readable, and relevantly applied. A great service for the church and beyond.

Adriaan C. Neele
Research Scholar, Yale Divinity School

A delightfully different romp through some occasionally unexpected corners of the Reformation, viewed from a unique perspective. In a scholarly but very readable manner, Gatiss sheds light on its theology, critical importance, and relevance for gospel ministry today.

Andrew Reid
Principal, Evangelical Theological College of Asia, Singapore

LEE GATISS

LIGHT after DARKNESS

HOW THE REFORMERS REGAINED, RETOLD AND RELIED ON THE GOSPEL OF GRACE

CHRISTIAN
FOCUS

Copyright © Lee Gatiss 2019

paperback ISBN 978-1-5271-0333-7
epub ISBN 978-1-5271-0402-0
mobi ISBN 978-1-5271-0403-7

First published in 2019
by
Christian Focus Publications Ltd,
Geanies House, Fearn, Ross-shire,
IV20 1TW, Scotland
www.christianfocus.com

A CIP catalogue record for this book is
available from the British Library.

Cover design by Rubner Durais

Printed and bound by
Bell & Bain, Glasgow.

CONTENTS

PREFACE

This is a book about how the Protestant Reformers of the sixteenth century regained, retold, and relied on the gospel of grace – and what we can learn from them. It looks at both the tragedies and the triumphs of the Reformation, the dark deeds as well as the noble heroics. It reminds us of the glorious truths which warmed the hearts and fired the souls of passionate and imperfect people, and how they tried to share the good news of Jesus Christ in their generation. My prayer is that it will strengthen and inspire passionate and imperfect Christians today to emulate their clarity, their courage, and their compassion for the lost. Hence the constant need to stop and reflect on the application of this history for today, and the emphasis on prayer.

These chapters began life as conference talks or lectures given during the great celebrations surrounding the 500th anniversary of the Reformation. Some of the material here started out as lectures for my students at Union School of Theology, and from Biola University. Chapter 5 is an expanded version of an article which was originally published in *Faith & Worship* (80, Lent 2017), and parts of other chapters have appeared online and in *Crossway* magazine and *Evangelicals Now* in different guises. I was also privileged to speak on these exciting subjects in a wide variety of settings all over the British Isles, in Edinburgh, Belfast, Dublin, London, Cambridge, Durham, Tunbridge Wells, Colchester, Eastbourne, Malvern, and Sheffield, as well as in the USA, Greece, and Chile. I learned something each time from interaction with astute and careful listeners, which I have tried to incorporate into these chapters.

For the glory of God and the good of his world, I pray that the Lord would raise up labourers for the twenty-first century to go out into his harvest field and continue to make disciples of all nations, the way Luther, Zwingli, Tyndale, Calvin, and Cranmer did in their days. May this little book be a spur and encouragement to them. Soli Deo Gloria.

LEE GATISS
Cambridge, England

Ulrich Zwingli and Truth in the Midst of Darkness

Post tenebras lux. After darkness, light. That is the motto of the Reformation.

Five hundred years ago Europe seemed to be in spiritual darkness. The light of the gospel had been obscured – by human traditions, by churchly powers and authorities, and by silly superstitions. But then the light of truth in the Bible broke through. Not just Martin Luther, but a generation of men and women rediscovered in a powerful way that we are saved solely and completely by faith in Christ's death on the cross. What poured forth was a wave of impassioned teaching, writing, and new church movements that radically altered not just the shape of the church, but the entire course of human history. Today, this is what we call 'the Reformation'.

A Violent Tragedy!

But wasn't the whole thing a tragedy? A united Western Christendom was suddenly torn apart by religious division and war. People were burned at the stake for questions of religion. Surely that was a nightmare?

Naturally we want to repudiate the violence of those times and must regret that there was and is division between churches. Ultimately, however, the Reformation clarified a necessary distinction between teaching that was leading people astray spiritually, and the more edifying teaching of the Bible, which was again released into the world in a language people could understand.

There were wars and executions, and a noble army of martyrs were tied with chains to a stake and then burned alive for their faith – for reading the Bible in English and teaching, against Rome, that salvation is by grace alone. When Roman Catholic Queen Mary ascended the throne in 1553, she tried to undo the Reformation in England. She earned her nickname Bloody Mary by burning around 300 leading Protestants, both men and women, as heretics – including the Archbishop of Canterbury, Thomas Cranmer.

Even in quiet corners like Switzerland there was trouble. Reformers like Calvin and Zwingli brought the Reformed faith to cities which democratically voted to embrace it. The Roman Catholic backlash was harsh – Zwingli died in battle as Catholic forces attacked the army of his adopted home, Zurich. They butchered him and burned him at the stake, and forcibly re-Catholicized whole swathes of the country.

Later, Elizabeth I reinstalled Protestantism as the operating system in England. But the Pope declared her a bastard heretic, an illegitimate Queen promoting a false religion. She was excommunicated and denied salvation. Anyone who obeyed her or recognized her as Queen was also excommunicated and denied salvation.[1] So all Roman Catholics suddenly became potential terrorists and assassins in the eyes of the state, because the Pope was essentially giving them permission to depose her from power, with his blessing. So it is no wonder, since the Spanish sent armadas and such things against her, that Jesuit priests were often executed in Elizabethan England, and of course we also later had the Gunpowder Plot of Guy Fawkes in 1605.

In 1618 a war broke out in Europe which would divide the continent for thirty years. The Catholic Holy Roman Emperor sought to re-establish his control over Protestant areas and was fiercely resisted. The Kingdom of Bohemia (in what is now the Czech Republic) elected a Protestant as its new king, and the Catholic Holy Roman Emperor was not happy about this. Dynastic politics were obviously involved too, and the great powers were all sucked into it. This Thirty Years War resulted in around eight million casualties.

Why did all this happen? As the Roman Catholic writer, Brad Gregory, says in his book on the execution of Christians during the sixteenth century: 'Christians so vehemently defended the doctrines that divided them *because of their shared convictions* about what was at stake. Christianity was not a tissue of human invention, but the authoritative response to God's revelation. It concerned not a disciplinary regime as such, but the right ordering of human life, individually and collectively,

---

1. See *Regnans in Excelsis* (1570) which can be accessed at http://www.papalencyclicals.net/Pius05/p5regnans.htm

such that eternal salvation remained possible.'[2] This was true for both sides. It's why they were willing to die and, sadly, to kill.

Both Protestants and Roman Catholics were convinced that the Christian faith is not ours to twist or mould according to our own preferences and desires. It is a revealed faith, spoken by God, and getting it wrong puts our eternal destiny at stake. It is only because many no longer believe in God or in eternity or in truth that our culture finds this so difficult to understand. The differences of five centuries ago are seen as minor and not worth suffering for, by a more secular age which cares more for establishing its own definitions of righteousness in the here and now than in living to please a benevolent Creator who promises life in a renewed world beyond death.

However, Europe was not an entirely peaceful place for the previous 1000 years of course. There had been an ongoing battle between Popes and Princes stretching back centuries, and various movements for reform and renewal of the church. Despite some superficial similarities, the Reformation was not an unfortunate 'Brexit' as a few have tried to make out, with England making a mess of a supposedly peaceful and prosperous harmony. Germany was divided; France was divided; Scandinavia was divided; as gospel light flooded all of Europe. As Jesus said: 'Do not think that I have come to bring peace to the earth' (Matt. 10:34). The truth may set you free, but it also divides.

---

2. Brad Gregory, *Salvation at Stake: Christian Martyrdom in Early Modern Europe* (London: Harvard University Press, 1999), 344.

LUTHER'S RESPONSIBILITY

None of this was directly or solely caused by Martin Luther himself or by Protestantism as such. One man did not cause all the ensuing deaths and devastation. Indeed, Luther explicitly repudiated violence as a means of spreading his ideas. Despite how some have portrayed him, he was not a Jihadi, thirsting for literal holy war against the Pope, or a terrorist intent on blowing up St Peter's Basilica in Rome. He said Christian love 'should not employ harshness here nor force the matter ... for it should be left to God, and his Word should be allowed to work alone ... I cannot, nor should I, force any one to have faith.'[3] Later he reflected: 'I opposed indulgences and all the papists, but never with force. I simply taught, preached, and wrote God's word; otherwise I did nothing.'[4]

Now, Luther wasn't always a paragon of virtue in his use of language against others. He also had something of a potty mouth. But he explicitly repudiated violence and force as a method for spreading the true faith. Still, he revelled in being an 'uncultivated fellow who has always moved in uncultivated circles.'[5] Some of the Pope's teachings were 'farts out of his stinking belly,' Luther asserted.[6] He could describe certain Roman Catholic institutions and practices with which he heartily disagreed as 'an illusion and an evil odour, stinking worse

---

3. *Luther's Works* (LW), American Edition (55 vols.; ed. Jaroslav Pelikan and Helmut T. Lehmann; St Louis: Concordia, 1955–1986), Volume 51, 75-6. Citations of this set are abbreviated throughout to LW followed by the volume and page numbers (e.g., LW 51:75-6).

4. LW 51:77.

5. LW 33:15.

6. LW 41:281.

than the devil's excrement.'[7] Although his opponents also used this kind of language about him, such charming rhetoric was hardly ecumenical or diplomatic.[8]

He was also anti-semitic. His first book on the Jews, in 1523, was not too bad: Jesus was a Jew; let's gently tell them the gospel and not persecute them.[9] This was 'greeted with joy by Jewish readers throughout Europe' according to Martin Bertram.[10] But twenty years later, jaded by the failure of that former policy to see the Jews converted to Christ, he wrote a dreadful book called *On the Jews and their Lies*.[11] Here he advocated persecution: burn down their synagogues, destroy their houses, remove their books, silence the rabbis, curtail their freedom of movement.[12] It is full of that filthy language I just mentioned too. He wasn't the only one who felt and wrote this way. He was a man of his times. As Carl Trueman rightly points out: 'Anti-Jewish polemic was not invented by Luther but had a longstanding and well-established pedigree, stretching back into the Middle Ages and beyond.'[13] But that is no

7. LW 38:187.

8. I have explored some of Luther's more colourful language in an article which my editor wouldn't let me call 'The 95 Faeces'; see 'When Scatology Informs Theology: The Bowels of the Reformation' at https://www.thegoodbook.co.uk/blog/interestingthoughts/2017/01/31/when-scatology-informs-theology-the-bowels-of-the-/.

9. See 'That Jesus Christ Was Born a Jew' in LW 45:197-230.

10. See Bertram's translator's introduction to 'On The Jews and Their Lies', in LW 47:124.

11. LW 47:123-306.

12. LW 47:268-70.

13. Carl Trueman, *Histories and Fallacies: Problems Faced in the Writing of History* (Wheaton: Crossway, 2010), 132.

excuse – he should have known better. The Bible, as well as his own earlier work, should have warned him against the move from theological anti-Judaism, into outright bigotry and violent language.[14]

It would be nice if we could all just get along despite our differences, wouldn't it? But the fault here does not lie with Protestantism, or even with religion as such of course. We must put it all into perspective. The great secular regimes of the twentieth century rejected Christianity altogether. Yet Nazi Germany, Soviet Russia, Communist China, and Pol Pot's Cambodia were not exactly paragons of peace, love, and harmony either for their own populations or on a world stage. There is a bigger picture we must take into account.

It is a tragedy that there was so much bloodshed in the sixteenth and seventeenth centuries, and religion was often a pretext for it. But that is part of a much longer story that goes back to the fall of the human race, and the first murder of Abel by his brother Cain – which graphically illustrated the depths of sin first introduced into the world by the rebellion of Adam and Eve (Genesis 3–4). Religion was not uninvolved in that primeval conflict either, but its real cause is ultimately the same as that which has brought such misery to the human race ever since we listened to the serpent and doubted God's word in Eden. Both Catholic and Protestant churches have had to recruit their members from a fallen human race.

---

14. See Trueman, *Histories and Fallacies*, 129-38 on how Luther's anti-Semitism was primarily religious and not biological or racial, and the difficulties with comparing it to Nazism.

Zwingli's Tragic Struggles

The Reformers regained and retold the gospel, but they also relied on God's grace themselves in very personal and direct ways. Another Reformer whose own actions, like Luther's, were both heroic and somewhat morally dubious is Ulrich Zwingli (1484-1531). He was a powerful Protestant preacher, but also a deeply flawed man.

For example, Zwingli and ten prominent clergy friends wrote to their bishop about clerical celibacy in 1522. The discipline of not allowing clergy to marry is without biblical mandate as a compulsory practice,[15] but has ancient roots from at least the fourth century. By the end of the tenth century it had become practically obsolete.[16] At the First Lateran Council in 1123, however, the Roman Catholic Church adopted rigorous canons against this practice.[17] Zwingli and his friends begged their bishop to relax the medieval rule, or at least permit them to flout it.[18] They were very keen to preach the gospel, they said, and were making vigorous efforts to do so. But they found keeping this rule of celibacy just too hard. They wrote:

15. See e.g., Matthew 8:14-15 and 1 Timothy 3:2.

16. Henry C. Lea, *History of Sacerdotal Celibacy in the Christian Church* (New York: Macmillan, 1907), 1.182, comments that 'Legitimate marriage or promiscuous profligacy was almost universal, in some places unconcealed, in others covered with a thin veil of hypocrisy according as the temper of the ruling prelate might be indulgent or severe.'

17. See Canons 3 and 21. See also Canons 6 and 7 of the Second Lateran Council (1139).

18. See 'Petition of certain preachers of Switzerland to the Most Reverend Lord Hugo, Bishop of Constance, that he will not … endure longer the scandal of harlotry, but allow the Presbyters to marry wives or at least would wink at their marriages,' in Samuel M. Jackson (ed.), *The Latin Works and Correspondence of Huldreich Zwingli: Volume 1* (London: G. P. Putnam's & Sons, 1912), 150-65.

> We, then, having tried with little enough success alas! to obey the law … have discovered that the gift [of celibacy] has been denied unto us, and we have meditated long within ourselves how we might remedy our ill-starred attempts at chastity.[19]

In other words, we've tried to keep our trousers on, but failed. 'But after that loathing of ourselves, through which we recognized at once our rashness and our weakness, the hope of a remedy began to show itself, though from afar.'[20] We should just get married! Scripture says nothing against that, so why won't you take a lead and show the way forward on this? 'From the whole vast crowd,' they said, 'we are the first to venture to come forward, relying upon your gentleness, and to implore that you grant us this thing.'[21] Was this uncommon courage, or ungodly carnal lust?

They openly confessed: 'We have been so on fire from passion with shame be it said ! that we have done many things unseemly.'[22] But actually, it is probably your fault as well, bishop (they implied), for insisting on clerical celibacy which the Bible and the early church never did. The Lutheran theologian, Philip Melanchthon (1497–1560), said that *voluntary* celibacy could be undertaken without sinning, but not if it was considered a meritorious work which makes us righteous. It was sinful for bishops to bind a Christian's conscience to

---

19. Jackson, *The Latin Works and Correspondence of Huldreich Zwingli*, 156.

20. ibid., 157.

21. ibid., 159.

22. ibid., 160.

something which God had not commanded, he wrote.[23] John Calvin later agreed, adding (in comments on 1 Tim. 4) that compulsory celibacy also 'set up a false and spurious worship of God.'[24]

So Zwingli and his friends earnestly pleaded with the bishop to do the right thing. 'We think,' they said, 'it [is] the duty of bishops ... to drive into marriage those whom they have detected in fornication. For fornication must be met, because besides exposing one to judgment it also offends one's neighbour. Influenced then by these passages we are at length persuaded that it is far more desirable if we marry wives, that Christ's little ones may not be offended, than if with bold brow we continue rioting in fornication.'[25]

A similar argument is sometimes employed by those who advocate same-sex marriage as an option for Christians. Would it not be better, they say, for same-sex partners to have open to them a form of marriage? Would this not hallow and direct aright the impulses and affections which they find within them, in a permanent, faithful, and stable form of relationship, much as heterosexual couples enjoy? Would this not

23. See *Apology of the Augsburg Confession*, Article XXVII.21-3. T. G. Tappert (ed.), *The Book of Concord: the Confessions of the Evangelical Lutheran Church* (Philadelphia: Mühlenberg Press, 1959), 272-3. Philip Melanchthon, *Common Places: Loci Communes 1521* (Translated by Christian Preus; St Louis, MO: Concordia, 2014), 188.

24. John Calvin, *Commentarius in Epistolam Pauli ad Timotheum I, et ad Timotheum II, et ad Titum.* Ioannis Calvini Opera quae supersunt omnia 52 (Edited by G. Baum, E. Cunitz, and E. Reuss; Brunswick: C. A. Schwetschke, 1863), 295.

25. Jackson, *The Latin Works and Correspondence of Huldreich Zwingli*, 162.

be preferable to some kind of dishonest cover-up, or the continuance of 'rioting in fornication' amongst those who are attracted to people of the same sex?[26] Zwingli would not agree to the extension of his logic here, however, because there is no biblical warrant for such marriages, and his whole point revolved around Scripture's specific remedy for his sexual struggles. All the same, one wonders if he and his friends might have explored the Christian doctrines of repentance and the mortification of sins just a little more.

Zwingli and his friends were very honest and open in their letter. It was a rhetorically powerful one too:

> For the sake of Christ the Lord of all of us, therefore, by the liberty won by his blood, by the fatherly affection which you owe to us, by your pity of our feeble souls, by the wounds of our consciences, by all that is divine and all that is human, we beseech you mercifully to regard our petition and to grant that which was thoughtlessly built up be thoughtfully torn down, lest the pile constructed not in accordance with the will of our Heavenly Father fall some time with a far more destructive crash.[27]

We may often be tempted to think of great religious men of the past as plaster-cast saints. Heroes, well beyond the struggles of our own day and age. But they were not. They were tragically flesh and blood, it seems. This wasn't an abstract issue for Zwingli either. He had secretly

---

26. See, for example, Jeffrey John, *Permanent, Faithful, Stable: Christian Same-sex Marriage* (Second Edition; London: Darton, Longman & Todd, 2012).

27. Jackson, *The Latin Works and Correspondence of Huldreich Zwingli*, 163.

married Anna Reinhard, a widow, and was living with her. Eventually, they had a public ceremony in 1524, just a few months after their first child was born.

Marriage is a gift of God, especially for those who are aflame with uncontrollable desire, according to Zwingli. For them, taking oaths of perpetual celibacy was foolish, and living (so to speak) beyond their means, when God had already offered a solution. 'Do you burn, then?' he wrote in 1525, 'Marry; for you do better and more rightly in quenching the flames of ungovernable passion by marrying than in carrying about a mind restless and filthy from burning. And how long you ought to bear the burning no man can tell better than yourself. There are very, very few in the whole number of mortals who do not burn; and I am not sure that there has at any time, to say nothing of today, been one who has not felt the fires of passion; but how fiercely each burns no one can know save Him to whom the heart is known.' Only you can decide when it is right to take a wife, he said, but he was very honest about what the struggle of singleness might be like until then: 'But you will take one when you see that nearly all your thoughts are carried away by the violence of this fire as by a torrent; that fear of God is thrown to the winds, love of him killed, prayer hindered.'[28] To ignore marriage in such a state, so as to prioritise a vow of celibacy, was 'overriding the law of God on account of human tradition.'[29]

---

28. C. N. Heller (ed.), *The Latin Works of Huldreich Zwingli: Volume 3* (Philadelphia: Heidelberg Press, 1929), 261 (from his *Commentary on True and False Religion*).

29. Heller (ed.), *The Latin Works of Huldreich Zwingli*, 265. He adds: 'I will say nothing of those vile and filthy things that the majority of monks secretly devise from uncontrollable passion, so that it is quite plain that

The bishop, however, was not particularly motivated to end clerical celibacy. In one year, apparently, in a diocese of 15,000 priests, there were 1,500 children born to those priests. They were fined 4 or 5 'gulden' for such offences, so this was actually a nice little money-spinner for the diocese, and an acceptable, large-scale practice.[30]

When Zwingli was at Einsiedeln between 1516 and 1518, a friend wrote to him from Zurich and said there was a vacancy there at the Great Minster, and it would be great to see a gospel preacher like him installed in this strategic location. A few weeks later, however, he wrote again saying that there had been some objections to Zwingli's name. One in particular bothered him, and it wasn't the rumour that his aptitude for the guitar made him an impure, worldly sort of man. Some were saying that Zwingli had wronged the daughter of a prominent citizen in Einsiedeln, and this made him unsuitable to take the role.

For centuries we had no idea what Zwingli said to that, until in the nineteenth century, a Zurich professor called Johannes Schulthess discovered Zwingli's letter written a couple of days later in reply. In this long-forgotten letter, Zwingli admitted that he had slept with the woman (a barber's daughter of some ill-repute already) and had fallen into temptation with other women before that

---

their hearts, and sometimes their bodies also, are defiled with fouler lusts than those living in wedlock; nay, are so vile that they cannot even be compared with respectable marriages. But, however filthy and foul they are, they fail to obey the law of God on account of their vow.'

30. See Jackson, *The Latin Works and Correspondence of Huldreich Zwingli*, 177, footnote 1.

in Glarus too. But, he claimed, this unchastity was now a thing of the past; hard study of Greek and Latin philosophers and theologians helped take the heat out of such sensual desires for him, he claimed.[31] This is the kind of thing Zwingli was up to whilst Luther was nailing the 95 Theses on the door of the Castle Church in Wittenberg.

Professor Schulthess was appalled by this, and thought that it would ruin Zwingli's reputation, and harm the cause of Protestantism if it got out. He showed it to one of his students and then placed it in the flame of a candle to burn it and destroy the evidence. However, at the last moment, he thought better of this approach. He snatched it out of the fire again, and said, 'Protestantism is the truth, in all circumstances.'[32]

Zwingli's letter did eventually satisfy the Minster's appointments committee, and he was elected to the senior post. Zwingli's lack of chastity was far from exceptional; one of the alternative priestly candidates was said to have fathered no less than six children![33] He was perhaps on a faltering growth curve in sanctification; Samuel Simpson sees his life at Einsiedeln as 'a marked improvement over his former life at Glarus' and speculates that he may have

---

31. See his letter to Heinrich Utinger (5 December 1518) in *Huldreich Zwinglis Sämtliche Werke: Volume 7* (Corpus Reformatorum 94) (Leipzig: Heinsius, 1911), 110-113.

32. The story is told in Oskar Farner, *Huldrych Zwingli: Seine Entwicklung zum Reformator, 1506-1520* (Zurich: Zwingli-Verlag, 1946), 2:298-9.

33. W. P. Stevens, *Zwingli: An Introduction to His Thought* (Oxford: Clarendon Press, 1992), 16. Samuel Simpson, *Life of Ulrich Zwingli: The Swiss Patriot and Reformer* (New York: Baker & Taylor Co., 1902), 72, cites a report that this other candidate also held a number of livings already, in plurality.

left the latter to escape its strong temptations.[34] Jim West writes that 'being ensnared by the village tart is not quite the same thing as pursuing various sexual conquests,' which is strictly true, but not an entirely satisfactory justification of his behaviour (nor very kind to the lady in question), and Zwingli was somewhat flippant about it in his letter. West also rightly adds, however, that this episode 'so troubled Zwingli that he regretted it his entire life, thoroughly repented of it, and never again engaged in such behavior.'[35]

WALKING IN THE LIGHT

As the *Thirty-nine Articles of Religion* say of original sin, 'this infection of nature doth remain, yea in them that are regenerated.' And yet, we may still want to affirm that 'Protestantism is the truth, in all circumstances', regardless of the worst behaviour of its most famous advocates. Should we cover up those tragic elements of the story of how the Reformation brought light after darkness?

> This is the message we have heard from him and declare to you: God is light; in him there is no darkness at all. If we claim to have fellowship with him and yet walk in the darkness, we lie and do not live out the truth. But if we walk in the light, as he is in the light, we have fellowship with one another, and the blood of Jesus, his Son, purifies us from all sin (1 John 1:5-7 NIV).

---

34. Simpson, *Life of Ulrich Zwingli*, 60-1.

35. Jim West, *'Christ Our Captain': An Introduction to Huldrych Zwingli* (Quartz Hill, CA: Quartz Hill Publishing House, 2011), 14. There is an English translation of some of the confessional letter here too. Cf. Simpson, *Life of Ulrich Zwingli*, 74-5.

These verses are important because they encourage us to live in the light of the truth since anything less will hinder our fellowship with one another and with God. And they remind us that only the blood of Jesus can purify us from sin: he is the inexhaustible fountain of purity and sanctification, and all we need. Truth and light are important in times when scandal hits the church.

Truth is not well served if evidence is shoved under the carpet or consigned to the flames in a mistaken belief that it might harm the truth. Neither is truth or justice served by attempting to keep things (and people) as quiet as possible in the hope that it will all go away. We must walk in the light, and (as the *Book of Common Prayer* puts it) neither dissemble nor cloak such sins. People love darkness because their deeds are evil (John 3:19), and too often we are tempted to keep hidden things which are better off exposed to the light and dealt with.

When there are allegations of abuse or of immorality, whether today or in the distant past, it is important to remember that God does not require cover ups. Indeed, covering up our sin is a recipe for inner paralysis. Cowering behind the fig leaf of an outward conformity or piety is not the way to be happy but the path of misery, groaning, and a conflicted conscience (see Ps. 32:3-5). As John Donne (1572–1631) preached: 'Sin is a serpent, and he that covers sin, does but keep it warm, that it may sting the more fiercely, and disperse the venom and malignity thereof the more effectually.'[36] So the only road

---

36. John Donne, *The Works of John Donne* (London: John W. Parker, 1839), 2:523.

to spiritual health is to confess (with the Prayer Book) that 'there is no health in us'.

It is especially important here to say that the Lord God Almighty doesn't need that kind of defence. It's common for abuses to be hushed up by means of an appeal to the positive attributes of an alleged perpetrator and their usefulness to 'the cause', whatever that may be. We see that in political scandals, when politicians or secular activists do reprehensible things but are not called out or stopped for many years because groupthink takes over and says, 'We mustn't lose this person, despite their transgressions, because it would damage our cause.'

We also saw this in the crises which engulfed the Roman Catholic Church over paedophilia amongst priests, for whom celibacy remains the rule and now more strictly enforced.[37] This was a kind of 'far more destructive crash' about which Zwingli warned. Evidence was buried and abusers simply moved elsewhere (often to offend again). The abusers were too long protected by people on the inside saying, 'Trust the hierarchy to deal with it; don't stir things up or you'll harm the church and all the good work we're doing.'

This is a form of collusion in which both Catholics and Protestants have been tempted to indulge. It comes out of and breeds the sort of culture that identifies the gospel itself, or God, with 'our institution' (insert the

---

37. In November 1563, the Council of Trent anathematised clerics who married despite making an oath of celibacy on the grounds that 'they have not the gift of chastity', saying God would not refuse the gift to those who asked for it rightly, or allow them to be tempted beyond what they could bear. Session 24, Canon 9.

name of whatever individual, church, or parachurch organization you like), which elevates that ministry and its leaders to an almost untouchable status because 'God's work must be defended'.

It doesn't always go spectacularly wrong; but it certainly can and often does. People drawing attention to wrongdoing can be made to feel as ungodly as the perpetrators and accused of 'distracting people from the gospel'. But Protestantism is the truth in all circumstances. The gospel is not served by cover ups, though those who suffer wrongdoing (or know about it) in Christian circles will too often keep quiet because they don't want to be seen as 'undermining God's work'. Or they are ostracized by others for daring to talk about it. Some try to close down conversations or control the reporting of such incidents for the same reasons, often putting pressure on newspaper reporters or even just on people who post on social media.

But Jesus said, 'The truth will set you free' (John 8:32). And so we walk in the light as forgiven sinners, with no need to pretend we are better than we are. That is how we serve the truth, even in the midst of scandal. And as I have written elsewhere: 'We should not excuse or ignore reprehensible behaviour in the heroes of the past, because to do so only encourages it in the heroes of the present (and their imitators).'[38] So, with Zwingli, let us pray:

> Lord, God Almighty, who by your Spirit has united us into your one body in the unity of the faith, and has commanded your body to give praise and thanks

---

38. Lee Gatiss, *Cornerstones of Salvation: Foundations and Debates in the Reformed Tradition* (Welwyn: Evangelical Press, 2017), 229.

unto you for that bounty and kindness with which you have delivered your only begotten Son, our Lord Jesus Christ unto death for our sins: grant that we may fulfil this your command in such faith that we may not by any false pretences offend or provoke you who are the infallible truth. Grant also that we may live purely, as becomes your body, your sons and your family, that even the unbelieving may learn to recognise your name and your glory. Keep us, Lord, lest your name and glory come into ill repute through the depravity of our lives.[39]

And as Luther also prayed:

Almighty God, the protector of all who hope in you, without whose grace no one is able to do anything, or to stand before you: Grant us your mercy in abundance, that by your holy inspiration we may think what is right, and through your power perform the same; for the sake of Jesus Christ our Lord.[40]

---

39. W. J. Hinke (ed.), *The Latin Works of Huldreich Zwingli: Volume 2* (Philadelphia: Heidelberg Press, 1922), 289 (from 'The Order of Service We Use at Zurich, Berne, Basel, and the Other Cities of the Christian Alliance'). I have updated the English a little.

40. See 'Almechtiger Gott, der du bist eyn beschutzer …' in Luther's German Mass, in *D. Martin Luthers Werke* (90 vols.; Kritische Gesamtausgabe; Weimar: H. Böhlau, 1883–), 19:86 (my translation).

WILLIAM TYNDALE AND LIGHT IN THE MIDST OF ERROR

It is easy to see why many people dislike the Reformation, if it was something to do with that nasty Luther or this immoral Zwingli. Not to mention those who say it all only happened because the lustful Henry VIII wanted a divorce! Was it all really necessary? Wasn't everything just fine already before 1517?

A RADICAL DISTORTION

The traditional view of the late medieval church was one of ignorance, corruption, and growing anti-clericalism replaced at the Reformation by the re-discovered gospel, vernacular Bibles and liturgies, and increased lay devotion. This has been challenged in recent years by (amongst others) Professor Eamon Duffy at Cambridge. His book, *The Stripping of the Altars*, painted a picture of a vibrant and beloved church unjustly attacked and stripped bare by Henry VIII and his Protestant successors.[1]

---

1. See Eamon Duffy, *The Stripping of the Altars: Traditional Religion in*

More recently, however, Professor G. W. Bernard, vice-president of the Royal Historical Society, published a searching examination of the late medieval church on its own terms.[2] This, I think, gives us a much more nuanced picture of what was going on. Bernard claims that much of the recent writing on this period, particularly of the Duffy 'school', does not tell the full story, and indeed leaves the subsequent Reformation 'inexplicable'. Yes, there was some vitality in the church of the Middle Ages, but within that there were serious and substantial vulnerabilities which have been ignored or played down. That is not to make the break with Rome and the eventual triumph of Protestantism in various places an absolute inevitability. Yet Bernard places provocative question marks over the revisionist accounts of late, and allows us to ask again what the proper criteria for judging the late medieval background to the Reformation should really be.

The nineteenth-century bishop, J. C. Ryle, in his usual, breezy Victorian way, also speaks about the religion of England before the Reformation. In the book *Distinctive Principles for Anglican Evangelicals*, he has a chapter on what we owe to the Reformation. In there he writes of the radical distortion of Christianity which was medieval religion:

> To sum up all in a few words, the religion of our English forefathers before the Reformation was

---

England 1400–1580 (London: Yale University Press, 2005) and his more recent *Saints, Sacrilege and Sedition: Religion and Conflict in the Tudor Reformations* (London: Bloomsbury, 2012).

2. See G. W. Bernard, *The Late Medieval English Church: Vitality and Vulnerability before the Break with Rome* (London: Yale University Press, 2012) and my review in *Theology* 116.5 (September 2013), 379-80.

a religion without knowledge, without faith, and without lively hope – a religion without justification, regeneration, and sanctification – a religion without any clear views of Christ or the Holy Ghost. Except in rare instances, it was little better than an organized system of Mary-worship, saint-worship, image-worship, relic-worship, pilgrimages, almsgivings, formalism, ceremonialism, processions, prostrations, bowings, crossings, fastings, confessions, penances, absolutions, masses, and blind obedience to the priests. It was a huge higgledy-piggledy of ignorance and idolatry, and serving an unknown God by deputy.[3]

He goes on to demonstrate how 'the Reformation delivered England from the most groveling, childish, and superstitious practices in religion.' Alluding specifically to the worship of relics, he recounts some of the most ridiculous examples, before he concludes: 'Wonderful as these things may seem, we must never forget that Englishmen at that time had no Bibles, and knew no better. A famishing man in sieges and blockades has been known to eat rats and mice and all manner of garbage, rather than die of hunger. A conscience-stricken soul, famishing for lack of God's word, must not be judged too hardly, if it struggles to find comfort in the most debasing SUPERSTITION. Only let us never forget that this was the superstition which was shattered to pieces by the Reformation. Remember that. It was indeed a deliverance.'[4]

---

3. J. C. Ryle, *Distinctive Principles for Anglican Evangelicals*, ed. Lee Gatiss (London: Lost Coin, 2012), 25.

4. Ryle, *Distinctive Principles*, 27.

Many were delivered from these things, only to have their bodies handed over to the flames. We must never forget how many suffered and died to establish the Reformation in this country. It is an axiom of Christian faith that 'God's power is made perfect in weakness' (2 Cor. 12:9). What people often mean for harm, God can turn to good (cf. Gen. 50:20). So it is, that in the tragedies of the Reformation era we can also observe its triumph. People died for the sake of the gospel they had regained.

This is powerfully illustrated for us in the accounts given in Foxe's book of martyrs.[5] Read there the stories of Archbishop Cranmer, who recanted his Protestantism, and then repented of his recantation as he went to the stake. Read of the deaths of good Bishop Ridley and good Bishop Latimer, who died together for their faith. Their stories are well known, or should be. They died to light a candle in England that would never be put out. Foxe also writes of some brave Protestant ladies:

> Now, when these previously mentioned good women were brought to the place in Colchester where they should suffer … they fell down upon their knees, and made their humble prayers unto the Lord: which thing being done, they rose and went to the stake joyfully, and were immediately chained to it; and after the fire had compassed them about, they with great joy and *glorious triumph* gave up their souls, spirits, and lives, into the hands of the Lord … Thus (gentle reader) God chooses the weak things of the world, to confound mighty things.[6]

---

5. John Foxe, *Actes and Monuments of these Latter and Perillous Days, Touching Matters of the Church* (1563) and later editions.

6. Foxe, *Actes and Monuments*, from Book 12, page 2021 of the 1583

TYNDALE AND THE ENGLISH BIBLE

What did this noble army of martyrs give their lives for? In the midst of their tragedies, we turn now to observe the glorious triumphs of the Reformation. That is what they died for. Reformation theology is sometimes summarized in five *solas*: it was about salvation by grace alone (*sola gratia*), through faith alone (*sola fide*), by Christ alone (*solo Christo*), which we know through Scripture alone (*sola scriptura*), and all to the glory of God alone (*soli Deo gloria*).

I'm not sure it was ever summarized quite so neatly at the time, and there were other issues of immense importance during the Reformation, which are not accounted for in this traditional outline. For example, many of our English Reformers went to the stake not for justification by faith alone, but because they said that the bread and wine in communion are bread and wine *alone*; and that in the Lord's Supper we feed on Christ *only* in our hearts by faith, not literally and physically.[7]

Yet clearly, when it comes to our understanding of Scripture and salvation, the traditional five *solas* are extremely important. Let's think here about *sola scriptura*, and the way the Reformation recovered the Bible for the church. The apostle Paul wrote: 'All Scripture is breathed out by God and profitable for teaching, for reproof, for correction, and for training in righteousness' (2 Tim. 3:16). This verse sums up why Protestants showed such holy enthusiasm for the Bible.

edition (emphasis mine), which is available online at www.johnfoxe.org (I have updated the English).

7. See Lee Gatiss (ed.), *Foundations of Faith: Reflections on the Thirty-nine Articles* (London: Lost Coin, 2018), 172-8, 194-207.

It is not so much in-spired as ex-spired, breathed out by God. But as well as being the word of God himself, the Bible is also a terrifically useful book; indeed, it was given to us in order that we might use it. It is an infallible and inerrant instrument for teaching, rebuking, correcting, and training us.

That's why the Reformers of the sixteenth century were so excited about the Bible – both translating it and teaching it. It is particularly why William Tyndale (1494–1536) spent such time and energy in the dangerous work of translating the Greek and Hebrew original texts into English, and smuggling them into England. There was a message from God that everyone needed to hear, in a language they could understand, not just faulty ancient Latin which was reserved for the elite. Tyndale is surely one of the greatest heroes of the English Reformation. John Foxe called him 'the apostle of England'.[8] A gifted scholar and courageous reformer, he spent his most productive years in exile on the continent, yet he had a deep and lasting impact on every parish in England. The truths which motivated him, and which led to his martyrdom, continue to present a challenge to every Christian and every local church.

As Ashley Null writes: 'Long before Luther, the leaders of English society were committed to a thorough reform and renewal of the medieval English church through an emphasis on the power of Scripture.'[9] John Wycliffe (1330–1384) for example, wrote that 'every Christian

---

8. Foxe, *Actes and Monuments* (1583), 8:1075.

9. Ashley Null and John W. Yates III (eds.), *Reformation Anglicanism: A Vision for Today's Global Communion* (Wheaton: Crossway, 2017), 54.

must be a theologian' and know Holy Scripture, particularly for evangelisation since 'it is necessary to preach all the way to the very ends of the earth.'[10] Reading the Bible in the vernacular was an essential way to correct abuses and false teaching in the church, he said.[11] William Tyndale, however, was the man who achieved more than anyone on this front.

Tyndale was a talented linguist. Martin Luther's friend Spalatin reported in his diary that the Englishman knew seven languages, and seemed amazingly fluent in them all.[12] It was this aptitude above all which made Tyndale so useful to the cause of the Reformation, because he made it his life's aim to translate the word of God into his mother tongue. Until then, the Bible was only really available here in an ancient Latin translation which most people could not understand. Portions of hand-copied translations from that Latin into middle English were seen in the hands of Lollard followers of John Wycliffe. But these were few and far between, fairly unintelligible, and often considered contraband. Tyndale wanted something better.

He first suggested the idea to the Bishop of London, and asked for the means to make it happen under the auspices of the established church hierarchy. He was

10. See John Wyclif, *On the Truth of Holy Scripture*, trans. Ian Christopher Levy (Kalamazoo, MI: Medieval Institute Publications, 2001), 285-306 especially 287, 291, 300.

11. John Wyclif, *Trialogus*, trans. Stephen E. Lahey (Cambridge: Cambridge University Press, 2013), 192 (*Trialogus* 3.31).

12. Henry Walter (ed.), *The Works of William Tyndale*, 2 vols. (Edinburgh: Banner of Truth, 2010), 1:xxx (originally from the Parker Society editions, first published in 1849 and 1850).

not only rebuffed, but when he did finally manage to publish an English New Testament, the Bishop led the way in opposing its spread. At first it sold well, as copies secretly made their way from Tyndale's base across the Channel. But in February 1526, thirty-six bishops, abbots, and priors stood outside St Paul's Cathedral and burned basketfuls of Protestant books, including Tyndale's New Testament.[13]

The Archbishop of Canterbury spent a large amount of money buying up every copy he could lay his hands on – not for distribution to those starving for want of the word, but in order to destroy them.[14] Undaunted at these seeming setbacks, Tyndale rejoiced – because this cash actually helped keep him and his smuggling operation alive and enabled him to pay for an improved edition of the book.

Why did Tyndale risk his life and livelihood? 'I had perceived by experience,' he said, 'that it was impossible to establish the lay-people in any truth, except the scripture were plainly laid before their eyes in their mother tongue, that they might see the process, order, and meaning of the text.'[15] He could read the Bible in Hebrew and Greek, and had come to know the liberating truth of salvation by grace alone through faith alone. He longed for his fellow-countrymen to see this themselves in God's word. If only they could read it for themselves and see the context! A supposedly learned theologian

---

13. *Works of William Tyndale*, 1.xxxi.

14. *Works of William Tyndale*, 1.xxxiii.

15. *Works of William Tyndale*, 1:394 from his preface to the Pentateuch (1530).

once told him that it would be better to be without God's laws than the Pope's. So little did they esteem the Bible in those days. Tyndale, full of godly zeal, replied that if God spared him he would cause a boy that drives the plough to know more of the Scriptures than that theologian.[16]

Those 'words of health and of eternal life'[17] as he called them could alone bring us into true fellowship with God. 'The Scripture is a light, to show us the true way,' he said. Yet the enemies of truth were quenching it, with smokey sophistry and tiresome traditions, 'juggling with the text,' as he put it, and 'expounding it in such sense as is impossible to gather of the text, if thou see the process, order, and meaning thereof.'[18] This is what moved him to translate the New Testament.

These 'false prophets' were beguiling churchgoers with their dodgy interpretations of the Bible, contrary to the meaning of the text. They were twisting the Scripture violently 'unto their carnal and fleshly purpose,' Tyndale claimed,[19] persecuting others in 'defending of lewd imaginations and fantasies'[20] in order 'to satisfy their filthy lusts.'[21] If only people could read the Bible for

---

16. *Works of William Tyndale*, 1.xix.

17. *Works of William Tyndale*, 1:389 from the preface to his first edition of the New Testament (1526).

18. *Works of William Tyndale*, 1.394 from his preface to the Pentateuch (1530).

19. *Works of William Tyndale*, 1:147 from *The Obedience of a Christian Man* (1528).

20. *Works of William Tyndale*, 1:398 from his prologue to Genesis (1530).

21. *Works of William Tyndale*, 1:393 from his preface to the Pentateuch (1530).

themselves, they would see how outrageous such 'wolfish tyranny'[22] was!

So it was not just to enable people to be saved, that Tyndale rendered the Bible into beautiful, eloquent English. 'Scripture is the touchstone that tries all doctrines,' he wrote, 'and by that we know the false from the true.'[23] So people need to have Scripture in their own language in order to defend themselves against error. It was not just sufficient to translate it either, but people needed help in order to understand what they were reading. So Tyndale also wrote introductions and commentaries on books of the Bible, explicitly to 'expel that dark cloud which the hypocrites have spread over the face of the scripture,' and 'to edify the layman, and to teach him how to read the scripture and what to seek therein,' but also so that they could answer those who twisted it.[24]

Not long after he was burned at the stake for such 'heresies', it became compulsory (by God's grace!) for every Church of England parish to display an English Bible. The laity must be established and equipped with God's word, and the clergy must know it better. But in a day and age when we have easy, unfettered access to numerous translations and tools for understanding the Bible, do the laity read it as avidly as they should? And do the clergy teach them to handle it well, so that they can not only feed themselves with truth daily, but defend themselves from error too?

---

22. *Works of William Tyndale*, 1:28 from *A Pathway into the Holy Scripture* (1525).

23. *Works of William Tyndale*, 1:398 from his prologue to Genesis (1530).

24. *Works of William Tyndale*, 2:144, from the prologue to his exposition of 1 John.

THE SCRIPTURES AT THE HEART OF THE CHURCH

It was for these reasons that Thomas Cromwell (of *Wolf Hall* fame) and Archbishop Thomas Cranmer made sure every church in the land was furnished with an English Bible. Cranmer said that 'the Scripture of God is the heavenly meat of our souls.' As he preached (in one of the Church of England's official Homilies), 'Let us diligently search for the well of life in the books of the Old and New Testament, and not run to the stinking puddles of men's traditions, devised by men's imagination, for our justification and salvation.' And 'These books therefore, ought to be much in our hands, in our eyes, in our ears, in our mouths, but most of all in our hearts.'[25]

One of the best things about the Reformation is not its big characters and dramatic events; it is the return of warm-hearted, pastorally applied, biblical preaching to the church. I discovered this recently for myself as I was putting together a devotional resource to help ordinary people read the Bible alongside the Reformers.[26] They were observant readers and gifted teachers of the word, with a passion for understanding and passing on the world-changing insights God had shown them there. As I dusted down their old commentaries to see if there was anything of value in them for today, I felt I had discovered hidden treasure.

The Reformers wanted to make sure that the church always kept the Bible at the heart of its life and doctrine.

---

25. Gerald Bray, *The Books of Homilies: A Critical Edition* (Cambridge: James Clarke, 2015), 7, 8.

26. Lee Gatiss (ed.), *90 Days in Genesis, Exodus, Galatians, & Psalms with Calvin, Luther, Bullinger & Cranmer* (London: Good Book Company, 2017).

The *Thirty-nine Articles of Religion* – the Church of England's Reformation confession of faith – contain this crystal clear emphasis. For example, in Article 6 they say, 'Holy Scripture containeth all things necessary to salvation: so that whatsoever is not read therein, nor may be proved thereby, is not to be required of any man, that it should be believed as an article of the Faith, or be thought requisite or necessary to salvation.'

Scripture is utterly sufficient, just as Paul also said in 2 Timothy 3. It alone makes us wise for salvation in Christ. It alone can light the way, and it contains everything we need for eternal life and present godliness. Nothing ought to be demanded of us which Scripture itself does not demand, and no burden imposed on us which is not imposed by Scripture. At one stroke this way of looking at things undercuts all the pardons, pilgrimages, priestcraft, relics and other erroneous doctrines of the late medieval church.

Some people try to appeal to tradition or to the teaching of the early church Fathers, as an alternative or supplement to this idea of *sola scriptura*. The Italian Reformer, Peter Martyr Vermigli, who played an important role in the English Reformation, denied this, writing:

> For even if all the Fathers shall consent among themselves, yet we will not do this injury to the Holy Spirit, that we should rather give credit to them than to the word of God. Indeed, the Fathers themselves would never want themselves to be so believed, as they have sufficiently testified in their writings that they will not have that honour to be given to them, but to the holy Scriptures alone. So those who appeal from the

> Scriptures to the Fathers, appeal to the Fathers against the Fathers.[27]

Part of the definition of the church, according to the English Reformers, was that it is 'a congregation of faithful men, in which the pure word of God is preached' (Article 19). And yet that church cannot 'ordain any thing that is contrary to God's word written, neither may it so expound one place of Scripture, that it be repugnant to another' (Article 20). This is triumphant Reformation doctrine: Scripture is our supreme, coherent, and consistent rule both for salvation and for ordering our lives together as the church – rather than the changeable diktats of merely human authorities.

Cranmer taught that 'God's holy word' is 'one of God's chief and principal benefits given and declared to mankind here on earth.' So, he exhorts us: 'Let us night and day muse and have meditation and contemplation in them; let us ruminate and, as it were, chew the cud, that we may have the sweet juice, spiritual effect, marrow, honey, kernel, taste, comfort and consolation of them.'[28] Yet are we content with milky sermonettes of ten minutes and a perfunctory fast-food daily diet? Only solid meat will bring solid reformation.

It is easy to give lip service to this idea, but to drag our heels and lag behind in our lives. As Luther said in his commentary on Paul's epistle to the Galatians:

---

27. Peter Martyr Vermigli, *The Common Places of the Most Famous and Renowned Divine Doctor Peter Martyr* (London: Henry Denham and Henry Middleton, 1583), 4:48-9 (I have updated the language).

28. Bray, *The Books of Homilies*, 12-13.

At the first, when the light of the gospel began to appear, after such a great darkness of human traditions, many were zealously bent to godliness. They heard sermons greedily and had the ministers of God's word in reverence. But now, when the doctrine of piety and godliness is happily reformed, with so great an increase of God's word, many which before seemed earnest disciples, become despisers and very enemies. They not only cast off the study of God's word, and despise its ministers, but also hate all good learning.[29]

It is worth searching our hearts on these points. Have we grown so accustomed to the great benefits given to us by the Reformation that we have started to take them for granted? The Bible is readily available in a multitude of English translations, freely available on the internet, on our phones, even on our iWatches. Yet are we in danger of drifting away from serious study of God's word and 'all good learning' because we have neglected to drink from these fountains of life and to value them as deeply as we ought? The writer to the Hebrews says: 'Therefore we must pay much closer attention to what we have heard, lest we drift away from it' (Hebrews 2:1).

Archbishop Cranmer also produced one of the most enduring legacies of the Reformation. In 1549 he first published the *Book of Common Prayer (BCP)*. The purpose of this was to enable the ordinary people of England to both hear God's word and to respond to him in prayer in their own heart language. No longer were priests hidden away behind rood screens with their backs to the congregation mumbling *hocus pocus* in Latin

---

29. See my *90 Days in Genesis, Exodus, Galatians, & Psalms with Calvin, Luther, Bullinger & Cranmer*, 18. Cf. LW 26:45f.

like a magical incantation. No more: *Pater noster qui es in caelis, sanctificetur nomen tuum.* No more *Credo in Deum Patrem omnipotentem, Creatorem caeli et terrae.*

You can teach a child to recite such Latin. My children could all do the Lord's Prayer in fluent ecclesiastical Latin from an early age. But it is another thing entirely to pray it from the heart. It was the Reformation which made it possible and normal for us to say, 'Our Father in heaven, hallowed be your name'; and to declare with feeling, 'I believe in God, the Father almighty, Creator of heaven and earth.'

Cranmer's prayer book sought in its beautiful, sonorous English words and in its simplicity of choreography, to teach the doctrines of Reformation faith. The BCP was a hugely effective evangelistic tool for a liturgical people. It was designed to teach those who were used to church and liturgy a more Reformed and Protestant way to approach God with freedom and confidence. This was a strategy which made a huge amount of sense in a time and culture where most people went to church every Sunday and holy day. Its majestic language passionately pleaded with people to engage their hearts in serving a merciful God who sent his Son to save wretched sinners by faith alone. It expounded that gospel and urged congregations to respond.[30]

CONTINUING DIVISIONS TODAY

So in the midst of all the tragic error, it is here that we also find the triumph of the Reformation – in the recovery, by God's grace, of Scripture in the life of the

---

30. See the final chapter, below.

church. But we do also find another dark tragedy; the division of the church. The Pope spoke recently about the Reformation, and said:

> We too must look with love and honesty at our past, recognizing error and seeking forgiveness, for God alone is our judge. We ought to recognize with the same honesty and love that our division distanced us from the primordial intuition of God's people, who naturally yearn to be one, and that it was perpetuated historically by the powerful of this world rather than the faithful people, which always and everywhere needs to be guided surely and lovingly by its Good Shepherd.[31]

He continued by acknowledging that, 'With gratitude we acknowledge that the Reformation helped give greater centrality to sacred Scripture in the Church's life.' And of Luther he said that, 'With the concept "by grace alone", he reminds us that God always takes the initiative, prior to any human response, even as he seeks to awaken that response.' His practical conclusion on that Reformation anniversary was that, 'we have a new opportunity to accept a common path ... Nor can we be resigned to the division and distance that our separation has created between us. We have the opportunity to mend a critical moment of our history by moving beyond the controversies and disagreements that have often prevented us from understanding one another.'

---

31. The Homily of His Holiness Pope Francis at Lund on Monday, 31 October 2016, available at https://w2.vatican.va/content/francesco/en/homilies/2016/documents/papa-francesco_20161031_omelia-svezia-lund.html.

The tragedy is that Rome, the entire Roman Catholic system centred on the Pope, failed then and fails now to grasp what it was really all about. Yes, we yearn to be one with all Christians. Indeed, we actually are – we are one with all true believers in Christ by faith, whatever institutional differences there may be between us. Faith alone is what unites us to Christ, not the Pope, not the Archbishop of Canterbury, not membership of any human organization. And united to Christ, the Good Shepherd, he will lead us as we hear his voice in the Scriptures, rejecting the 'stinking puddles' of human traditions and false authorities.

God does not simply take the initiative and then hope that this will awaken a response in us. There will be no response unless he regenerates us and we are born again. Until that happens, all we can do is sin, said Luther (as we will explore in the next chapter). 'We have no power to do good works pleasant and acceptable to God, without the grace of God by Christ preventing us [going before us], that we may have a good will, and working with us, when we have that good will,' says Article 10 of the Church of England's *Thirty-nine Articles*.

We cannot walk a common path with those who reduce the power of God's grace or make Scripture sit alongside Tradition as a rival authority. We cannot move beyond these controversies because they are the hinge on which everything turns, the vital spot. They exist precisely because we do understand each other, or at least, we have done in the past. There is no point at all in creating such vagueness about these things that we can pretend we actually agree about them after all, when we don't.

The gospel created the divisions of the sixteenth century – not the Protestants who rejected the superstitions and tyrannies of the past, and not even the powerful elites who wanted to maintain the status quo by persecuting them. What happened is this: Light came into the world, but people loved the darkness, and acted accordingly. A familiar story – and a gut-wrenchingly painful one at times. We overcome the darkness with love and patience, and by shining the light of the gospel into it, not pretending that the shade is not too bad after all.

Conclusion

The Reformers of the sixteenth century read God's word, translated it into a language ordinary people could understand, and wrestled with the big issues that still face followers of Christ today. Christians today serve the same Lord Jesus in their everyday lives and ministries as these great Reformers did in theirs, and continue to struggle as they did to keep his word first in their hearts and in their churches.

Another great slogan sometimes used in relation to the Reformation was *ecclesia reformata semper reformanda secundum verbum Dei* – Reformed churches are always in need of being reformed by the word of God. That is, we must not rest on our laurels, but continue going back to the Bible in each generation. The same truths that changed the course of history 500 years ago are still capable of changing lives today as people turn to Christ alone for their salvation, identity, and hope, in repentance and faith.

Despite the lamentable tragedies of that era, we must be thankful to God for those who lived by this motto in centuries gone by – for the clarity of their testimony to the truth, often sealed with their blood. I pray that it would again be heard – loud and clear – in and through all our churches, but especially through the Church of England today. That church regularly remembers William Tyndale, who was burned at the stake for translating the Bible into English, on 6 October 1536. Their Collect for his day is this:

> Lord, give to your people grace to hear and keep your word that, after the example of your servant William Tyndale, we may not only profess your gospel but also be ready to suffer and die for it, to the honour of your name; through Jesus Christ your Son our Lord, who is alive and reigns with you, in the unity of the Holy Spirit, one God, now and for ever.

MARTIN LUTHER AND THE GOSPEL
OF FREEDOM

In 2017, there were many celebrations of the 500th anniversary of 'The Reformation'. What we were actually celebrating, however, was the 500th anniversary of one particular work by Martin Luther: the 95 Theses. Or to give the work its proper title: *A Disputation on the Power of Indulgences*. This single work is often seen as the spark which lit the fire, the beginning of the Reformation. Michael Reeves calls it a freedom movement.[1]

Luther was hoping to start a debate. That's what 'theses' are in this context – brief propositions put forward to be debated and discussed in an academic forum (rather than a sustained argument developed over 80-100,000 words, which is what a modern academic *thesis* often is!). They were, essentially, ninety-five provocative tweets or Facebook status updates designed to get people talking and make points about the gospel. Yet it turned out to be less than good news for Luther, in the short term. All this began the process in which he would end up being

---

1. See Michael Reeves, *Freedom Movement* (Leyland: 10Publishing, 2017).

tried for heresy, spend many months as a prisoner in a castle, and eventually be excommunicated by the Roman Catholic Church four years later.

There are two things we should note about this whole affair. First, the 95 Theses was not Luther's first publication. He had been writing and speaking and publishing theological works for several years by this point. We'll look at what else he wrote, in a moment. Second, Luther did not consider the issue of indulgences to be the defining issue of the Reformation. In his debate with Erasmus on the issue of free will and salvation, Luther said this to the Dutch humanist:

> I praise and commend you highly for this, that unlike all the rest you alone have attacked the real issue … You have not wearied me with irrelevancies about the papacy, purgatory, indulgences, and such like trifles (for trifles they are rather than basic issues) … You and you alone have seen the question on which everything hinges, and have aimed at the vital spot.[2]

Indulgences were an irrelevance, Luther claimed. The Papacy – the role of the Pope in the church – was a small, trifling matter he said. The question on which everything hinges was this: are we saved by grace alone, or not? That is the really important subject. How can we be free?[3] So indulgences were just the presenting issue – the first, troublesome symptom of a more deeply worrying problem. So to really understand

---

2. LW 33:294.

3. I have looked in detail at Luther's debate with Erasmus in 'The Manifesto of the Reformation' in *Cornerstones of Salvation: Foundations and Debates in the Reformed Tradition.*

what Luther was about we need to take a longer and wider view.

LONGING FOR TRUE FREEDOM
So let's consider the road to October 1517.

Luther was ordained as a minister in 1507. He moved a year later to the newly created university in Wittenberg. He did a degree in the Bible, and then another in theology. By 1512 he had his PhD in theology and had joined the faculty of the university. By the autumn of 1516, Luther had already published some of his lectures on the Psalms, and his lectures on Paul's epistle to the Romans. In those notes on Romans he says that we stand before God 'but not by your own strength, no, only by faith in Christ'.[4] He speaks about how the righteousness of God is revealed by faith alone, and how 'by the righteousness of God we must not understand the righteousness by which He is righteous in Himself, but the righteousness by which we are made righteous by God. This happens through faith in the Gospel.'[5]

These are crucial exegetical insights for Luther's Reformational trajectory. The Reformation took shape in his mind as he reflected on Scripture, so Scripture was in a sense setting the agenda. Indeed, when he later told the story of his own spiritual journey, he commented especially on his insights into one particular verse, Romans 1:17: 'in the gospel the righteousness of God is revealed.' He said he used to hate this idea of 'the righteousness of God', because he understood that it was

---

4. LW 25:100.

5. LW 25:151.

about God rightly punishing us. But when he understood that Paul here was not talking about that, he says: 'Here I felt that I was altogether born again and had entered paradise itself through open gates … Thus that place in Paul was for me truly the gate to paradise.'[6]

In 1517, Luther was also working on the epistle to the Hebrews. He says in his lectures on Hebrews that 'those who contrive to blot out sins first by means of works and labors of penance err greatly.' They try to follow the example set by Christ when really they need to begin with the fact that Christ suffered and died for them.[7] Later he adds:

> This is the crossroad where the truly righteous and the hypocrites separate. For those who are truly righteous press forward to works through faith and grace; the hypocrites, with perverse zeal, press forward to grace through works, that is, to what is impossible. But that endless tradition of decretals, decrees, statutes, etc., has multiplied us work-righteous hypocrites like 'locusts out of the smoke,' as Rev. 9:3 writes, and thus has darkened for us the sun of the completely pure faith, so that the spirit also sobs anew for the church.[8]

So he is already developing, in his early lectures and comments on the biblical texts, a theology of

---

6. LW 34:337.

7. LW 29:124. This is the problem with many sermons which call on us to love others as Christ did (as if the power of human love was all we needed), but don't tell us about the forgiveness we require when we inevitably fail (which was achieved by Christ's loving sacrifice of himself on the cross) or the power to love available from the Spirit of Christ for those who repent and believe.

8. LW 29:232.

justification by faith alone, in deliberate contrast to the whole penitential system of the Roman Catholic church in his day. He wasn't merely preparing lectures. He was recovering the gospel. He was preparing the way for Reformation.

More than a month before the 95 Theses, Luther published another set of propositions for academic debate: the disputation against scholastic theology. These ninety-seven theses (!) started to develop some of the key themes of Luther's work. Luther was not the only one at the time to ridicule certain scholastics for their 'worthless and mischievous intellectual gymnastics' as James Atkinson calls them.[9] He attacked them in the name of common sense, but also because Scripture was pushing him away from their false subtleties.

In the disputation against scholastic theology, he seemed to be reflecting on Romans 8:7-8: 'For the mind that is set on the flesh is hostile to God, for it does not submit to God's law, indeed, it cannot. Those who are in the flesh cannot please God', and on Romans 14:23: 'Whatever does not proceed from faith is sin.' Hebrews 11:6 may also have been in his mind: 'Without faith it is impossible to please God.' The texts he had studied and lectured on, fed into his critique of scholastic theology in the academy, and popular theology in the pews.

This led him to say that 'Hope does not come from earning merits.'[10] We are not called simply 'to do what

9. James Atkinson (ed.), *Luther: Early Theological Works* (London: Westminster John Knox Press, 1962, 2006), 262.

10. Thesis 25 of the *Disputation against Scholastic Theology*. See *Early Theological Works*, 268.

lies in us', to do our best and leave to God the rest. That's what the popular scholastic theology of the day said: *facientibus quod in se est, Deus non denegat gratiam* (to those who do what is in them, God will not deny grace).[11] Not so, said the early Luther. We are slaves to sin, branches cut from a corrupted tree, who cannot be made righteous simply by doing righteous deeds. Why? Because, 'Even a work which to all outward appearances … is a good work, the natural man in the secret recesses of his heart glories in it and takes a pride in it.'[12] It may look good on the outside and be a work of stunning quality to worldly eyes, 'but inwardly it is sin,' says Luther.[13] As Richard Rex rightly says, this insistence put Luther 'in a different theological world from both Erasmian humanism and scholastic Catholicism.'[14]

I highlight this particularly because it has a contemporary importance. There is a lot of discussion at the moment about certain sexual relationships which are considered harmful and offensive to God by Scripture. Many people would like not only to legalize gay marriage (which the state has done in many places), but also to say that gay marriage is not a sin anymore – because we now realize (apparently) that sexually active

---

11. See Heiko Augustinus Oberman, *The Harvest of Medieval Theology: Gabriel Biel and Late Medieval Nominalism* (Durham, NC: Labyrinth Press, 1983), 132-4 and his '*Facientibus quod in se est Deus non denegat Gratiam*: Robert Holcot, O.P. and the Beginnings of Luther's Theology' in *Harvard Theological Review*, 55.4 (October 1962), 317-42.

12. Thesis 37, *Early Theological Works*, 269.

13. Thesis 76, *Early Theological Works*, 271.

14. Richard Rex, *The Making of Martin Luther* (Oxford: Princeton University Press, 2017), 154.

homosexual relationships can display certain virtues in their permanence, faithfulness, and stability.

The Archbishop of Canterbury, for example, voted in Parliament *against* legalising gay marriage, but he also said that he is challenged by the 'stunning quality' of some gay relationships. Church of England documents have also said that such relationships can embody 'crucial social virtues', e.g.

> We are conscious that within both Church and society there are men and women seeking to live faithfully in covenanted same sex relationships. As we said in our response to the consultation prior to the same sex marriage legislation, 'the proposition that same sex relationships can embody crucial social virtues is not in dispute. Same sex relationships often embody genuine mutuality and fidelity ... two of the virtues which the Book of Common Prayer uses to commend marriage. The Church of England seeks to see those virtues maximised in society'.[15]

Tim Farron, the former leader of the Liberal Democrat party in the U.K., was rather cruelly hounded on the subject of sex during a recent election campaign, because he is a Christian. (Though why does one not see Muslim candidates quizzed on this subject in the same way?) Surely whether something is a sin or not is up to God, not up to our politicians, our journalists, or our

---

15. This phrase first appeared, I think, before same-sex marriage was legalised, in 'A Response to the Government Equalities Office Consultation – "Equal Civil Marriage" – from the Church of England', para. 9 (cf. also para. 14). Then it has been repeated in, for example, the House of Bishops Pastoral Guidance on Same Sex Marriage (February 2014) quoted here, and 'Marriage and Same Sex Relationships after the Shared Conversations' (GS 2055) in January 2017.

comedians on TV. In 2015 Mr Farron was asked whether he believed gay sex was a sin, and he replied: 'We're all sinners.' Which of course is right, as far as Romans and the rest of the Bible is concerned. But then, after a further barrage of questions, he said that he didn't think gay sex was a sin after all. Since resigning as party leader, he has expressed regret for this *volte face*. It would be outrageous in today's media culture, of course, to stand for office while saying that gay sex is a sin, because it is widely considered an unquestionable good, a freedom to be proudly celebrated. Moreover, politicians don't want to get into theology on prime-time TV.

What does one say to all this? It is true that certain ways of life can appear to display certain virtuous characteristics, of love and service. But that doesn't mean they are not at heart sinful ways of life. For example, we say 'there is honour amongst thieves'. A gang of robbers or pirates can be good friends to each other, be courageous and loyal and clever and persistent. We admire and cheer for *Ocean's Eleven*, the con artists from the TV show *Hustle*, and even Gru in *Despicable Me* when he and his minions steal the moon. But robbery is still theft.

I was speaking at a conference in Chile about this and other aspects of Reformation theology in 2017, when someone stole my computer. It was plugged in and providing the slides on the big screen when it suddenly disappeared from the front of the venue, five minutes before I was due to speak. There were hundreds of people there, and no one in the whole place saw the person do it, and the cameras transmitting live on YouTube did not catch them red-handed.

Now, let me tell you, I admire that kind of sneaky boldness! Don't you? Not that I'm encouraging anyone to try the same trick again. Still, I hope whoever it was who stole my laptop enjoys reading all the sermons on my hard drive, and listening to all the talks and lectures on Christian theology I had downloaded. As I've thought about it, I've also wondered whether maybe it was a man who felt he needed my laptop, to sell it, to feed his family; so what he rather brazenly and audaciously did could have been motivated by a paternal sense of responsibility (a crucial social virtue). But it was still a sin – and a jolly annoying and inconvenient one too.

Luther says, as the Bible says, that without faith it is impossible to please God. 'We maintain,' he said, 'that man without the Holy Spirit is completely ungodly before God, even if he were adorned with all the virtues of all the heathen.'[16] So whatever outward social virtues we may appear to exhibit in our lives, it does not ultimately matter.[17] All our righteous deeds are like filthy rags in God's sight unless we have at our core a love for Jesus and a desire to please him by faith alone. Until we submit to Jesus, we are hostile to God and cannot please him. No lifestyle which rejects the word of God can ever make

---

16. LW 2:42. 'In the historical accounts of the heathen there are certainly outstanding instances of self-control; of generosity; of love toward fatherland, parents, and children; of bravery; and of philanthropy.'

17. Luther does acknowledge that social virtues without the Spirit may matter in a certain limited sense: 'A difference must be made between civil affairs and theology,' he wrote, 'God gives his approval to the governments of the ungodly; he honours and rewards excellence even in the ungodly. Yet he does this so far as this present life comes into consideration, not the future life. And reason does have an understanding of what things are good as far as the state is concerned' (LW 2:42).

him smile, however brightly some sparks of common grace might seem to shine within it.

That is why authentic Reformation theology says that 'concupiscence and lust hath of itself the nature of sin' (Article 9 of the *Thirty-nine Articles*) and that 'the condition of Man after the fall of Adam is such, that he cannot turn and prepare himself, by his own natural strength and good works, to faith, and calling upon God: Wherefore we have no power to do good works pleasant and acceptable to God, without the grace of God by Christ preventing us,[18] that we may have a good will, and working with us, when we have that good will' (Article 10). The first book of Homilies speaks of 'how evil we be of ourselves; how of ourselves and by ourselves we have no goodness, help, nor salvation; but contrariwise, sin, damnation and death everlasting … for in ourselves, as of ourselves, we find nothing whereby we may be delivered from this miserable captivity … of ourselves and by ourselves we are not able either to think a good thought or work a good deed.'[19] Indeed, Article 13 of the *Thirty-nine Articles* states that such supposed good works which are 'not done as God hath willed and commanded them to be done, we doubt not but that they have the nature of sin.'[20]

The Westminster Confession also summarises this classic Protestant position. It says that there may be things that unregenerate people do which God commands,

---

18. That is 'going before' us, from the Latin *praevenire*.

19. See Bray, *The Books of Homilies*, 19-20.

20. For an exposition of these key Articles, see Lee Gatiss (ed.), *Foundations of Faith: Reflections on the Thirty-nine Articles* .

and which are socially useful, both to themselves and to others around them. However, 'because they proceed not from a heart purified by faith; nor are done in a right manner, according to the word; nor to a right end, the glory of God; they are therefore sinful and can not please God, or make a man meet to receive grace from God.' That is not to say, however, that it is perfectly fine for unbelievers not to display crucial social virtues, particularly since 'their neglect of them is more sinful, and displeasing unto God.'[21]

This is where Luther was also at, even before those famous 95 Theses on indulgences. He saw that the depths of sin in our hearts are so great, that in and of ourselves we can never be truly free. We cannot even see the kingdom of God unless we are born again (John 3:3).

AFTER THE 95 THESES

After the 95 Theses, Luther would continue to publish.

Another excellent disputation appeared in 1518, for a debate he had in Heidelberg. He repeats there the same emphasis on the stunningly useless quality of our secular social virtues: 'Although the works of man always seem attractive and good, they are nevertheless likely to be mortal sins,' he declared.[22] Luther also wrote a commentary on the 95 Theses, explaining and unpacking them further as well as publishing some sermons and his first set of lectures on Galatians in 1519.

---

21. *Westminster Confession of Faith*, 16:7. See also the *Belgic Confession*, Article 14, and the *Heidelberg Catechism*, Question 8, which says that unless we are regenerated by the Spirit of God, 'we are so corrupt that we are wholly incapable of doing any good and are inclined to all wickedness.'

22. LW 31:39.

Then in the second half of 1520, we get three of Luther's most important Reformation writings.[23] First, his address *To the Christian Nobility of the German Nation Concerning the Reform of the Christian Estate*. He attacked the inability of the Roman church to reform itself, and encouraged the aristocracy to do the job instead. Then second, *The Babylonian Captivity of the Church*, in which Luther angrily calls the Pope the Antichrist, and goes about reforming his understanding of the sacraments. The sacraments are reduced from the Catholic seven down to two – baptism and the Lord's Supper – while the cup is restored to the laity, transubstantiation is rejected, and the idea that the Mass is a meritorious good work and a sacrifice, is refuted.

Luther complained of the tyranny of the Pope (and 'the papists'), saying: 'Unless they will abolish their laws and ordinances, and restore to Christ's churches their liberty … they are guilty of all the souls that perish under this miserable captivity, and the papacy is truly the kingdom of Babylon and of the very Antichrist.'[24] As one commentator puts it, Luther's book on the Babylonian Captivity of the Church is 'a plea for spiritual religion and the liberty of the individual Christian as against mediaeval sacerdotalism and the mediaeval priestly caste.'[25]

Finally, of the three great early Reformation writings of Luther, we get *The Freedom of a Christian*. This was

---

23. They are sometimes called 'The Reformation Manifestos of 1520'. James Mackinnon, *Luther and the Reformation*, 4 vols. (London: Longmans, Green and Co, 1928), 2:222.

24. LW 36:72.

25. Mackinnon, *Luther and the Reformation*, 260.

addressed to the Pope himself, just a few months before Luther was finally excommunicated. It was not such an angry or polemical book, but more an attempt to present a summary of the Christian life as Luther had come to understand it.

All of this, then, is by Luther the Catholic – Luther before he was excommunicated.

LIBERTY!

The interesting thing about the last two pieces is that they have a common theme, liberty. The church needs to be free of the Babylonian captivity of the antichristian Pope. And the Christian is free, by faith alone. However, if we delight in the Reformation – which was all about being justified by faith alone and liberated – why are Reformation Christians often known more today for our traditionalism and insistence on rules? What can Luther teach twenty-first-century Christians about Christ 'whose service is perfect freedom' (as the Prayer Book puts it)?[26]

In *The Freedom of a Christian*, Luther 'released the word freedom (*libertas*), to ring through Europe and excite a bewildering variety of reactions in its hearers' according to Diarmaid MacCulloch.[27] It is a book about justification by faith alone: emancipation from the slavery of sin and liberty for sinners. Indeed, Richard Rex says that it is here that 'justification by faith alone was set out more clearly than ever before, along with the

---

26. The Second Collect, for Peace in the service of Morning Prayer.

27. Diarmaid MacCulloch, *The Reformation: Europe's House Divided 1490–1700* (London: Penguin, 2004), 131.

priesthood of all believers.'[28] Luther said of this book that, 'it contains the whole of Christian life in a brief form.'[29] His main point is contained in a double proposition. He says: 'A Christian is a perfectly free lord of all, subject to none. A Christian is a perfectly dutiful servant of all, subject to all.'[30]

We are perfectly free, and yet servants of all. He derives this seemingly paradoxical teaching from the Bible itself of course. In 1 Corinthians 9:19, Paul says: 'For though I am free from all, I have made myself a servant to all.' And in Romans 13:8 he writes that we are to 'Owe no one anything, except to love each other.' Even Christ, he says, though he was God, took the very nature of a servant (Phil. 2:6-7).

As he starts to unpack this, Luther looks at the twofold nature of humanity: we are body and soul. External things cannot affect the soul; if I eat well, or if I don't, it makes no difference to my soul – only to my body.[31] In the same way, 'It does not help the soul if the body is adorned with the sacred robes of priests or dwells in sacred places or is occupied with sacred duties or prays, fasts, abstains from certain kinds of food.' Even wicked people can do those things and perform such duties. 'On

---

28. Rex, *The Making of Martin Luther*, 152.

29. LW 31:343.

30. LW 31:344.

31. He is not thinking here of the sense in which what I do with my body can have spiritual consequences. For example, greed and drunkenness can exclude people from the kingdom of God (see Galatians 5:19-21 or Ephesians 5:5) while illicit sexual activity has more than merely physical effects according to Paul in 1 Corinthians 6, although it is also peculiarly damaging to oneself.

the other hand, he adds, 'it will not harm the soul if the body is clothed in secular dress, dwells in unconsecrated places, eats and drinks as others do, does not pray aloud, and neglects to do all the above-mentioned things which hypocrites can do.'[32]

What he is getting at is that the only thing necessary for a Christian life of righteousness and freedom is the word of God. The soul is powerless without the word. 'Therefore it is clear,' says Luther, 'that, as the soul needs only the word of God for its life and righteousness, so it is justified by faith alone and not any works; for if it could be justified by anything else, it would not need the word, and consequently it would not need faith.'[33]

So there it is: justification by faith alone. The heartbeat of Luther's gospel. Once you come to faith, says Luther, 'you learn that all things in you are altogether blameworthy, sinful, and damnable' – or as Paul says: 'All have sinned and fall short of the glory of God' (Rom. 3:23). You cannot get right with God by your own merits. So 'you are justified by the merits of another, namely, of Christ alone.'[34] True freedom is something we can only find in him.

So here we have two Reformation solas: *sola fide* and *solo Christo*. Justification by faith alone through the merits of Christ alone. We learn of this in the word of God, the Bible. As he says: 'If a touch of Christ healed, how much more will this most tender spiritual touch,

---

32. LW 31:345.

33. LW 31:346.

34. LW 31:346-7.

this absorbing of the word, communicate to the soul all things that belong to the word.'[35]

Faith does three things, according to Luther. First it justifies. It makes us right with God when we believe his word and grasp hold of it. Then, secondly, faith obeys. Because Christian liberty 'does not induce us to live in idleness or wickedness.'[36] We obey Christ, by faith alone, doing what he says – not because we hope to be saved by the merit of our works, but because we trust his word is true and right and good. As Luther summarizes it later: 'If a man were not first a believer and a Christian, all his works would amount to nothing and would be truly wicked and damnable sins.'[37] That is quite a shock.

We are not, however, to go to the other extreme. This doctrine does not leave us empty-mouthed, with nothing to say about social ethics. We are not to become antinomians, and think that simply by rejecting good works of all kinds we are somehow serving God.[38] Rather, Luther says: 'I will therefore give myself as a Christ to my neighbour, just as Christ offered himself to me.'[39] We are not saved by demonstrating crucial social virtues, but by Christ alone, who then enables us by his Spirit to live faithful lives of social virtue.

Third, faith not only justifies and obeys, it also unites us to Christ. Here, Luther uses the beautiful metaphor of a husband and wife: faith 'unites the soul with Christ as a bride is united with her bridegroom,' he says. This spiritual marriage causes a great exchange:

> Christ is full of grace, life, and salvation. The soul is full of sins, death, and damnation. Now let faith come between them and sins, death, and damnation will be Christ's, while grace, life, and salvation will be the soul's; for if Christ is a bridegroom, he must take upon himself the things which are his bride's and bestow upon her the things that are his. If he gives her his body and very self, how shall he not give her all that is his? And if he takes the body of the bride, how shall he not take all that is hers? … By the wedding ring of faith he shares in the sins, death, and pains of hell which are his bride's. As a matter of fact, he makes them his own and acts as if they were his own and as if he himself had sinned; he suffered, died, and descended into hell that he might overcome them all.[40]

He goes on and describes this as a 'royal marriage', in a dramatic picture which is worthy of any Disney movie:

> Here this rich and divine bridegroom Christ marries this poor, wicked harlot, redeems her from all her evil, and adorns her with all his goodness. Her sins cannot now destroy her, since they are laid upon Christ and swallowed up by him. And she has that righteousness in Christ, her husband, of which she may boast as of her own and which she can confidently display alongside her sins in the face of death and hell and say, 'If I have sinned, yet my Christ, in whom I believe, has not sinned, and all his is mine and all mine is his.'[41]

---

40. LW 31:351-2.

41. LW 31:352.

So the gospel is a romance. A hopeless, sinful slave marries the beautiful, powerful Lord. As Raymond Ortlund has also beautifully summarised it:

> Pastorally, the biblical story lifts up before us a vision of God as our Lover. The gospel is not an imperialistic human philosophy making overrated universal claims: the gospel sounds the voice of our Husband who has proven his love for us and who calls for our undivided love in return. The gospel reveals that, as we look out into the universe, ultimate reality is not cold, dark, blank space; ultimate reality is romance. There is a God above with love in his eyes for us and infinite joy to offer us, and he has set himself upon winning our hearts for himself alone. The gospel tells the story of God's pursuing, faithful, wounded, angry, overruling, transforming, triumphant *love*. And it calls us to answer him with a love which cleanses our lives of all spiritual whoredom.[42]

Luther's opponents such as John Eck attacked him as a heretic because he (allegedly) 'lacerated and falsified the text'. Eck railed against him: 'Nowhere does it say that the just man lives by faith alone.' Faith is a work, and works are not nothing just because they don't merit grace.[43] But Eck had completely missed the point, and not just of a few scattered texts. He had missed the glorious romantic plotline of the entire Bible.

---

42. Raymond C. Ortlund, *Whoredom: God's Unfaithful Wife in Biblical Theology* (Leicester: Apollos, 1996), 173.

43. John Eck, *Enchiridion of Commonplaces against Luther and Other Enemies of the Church* trans. Ford Lewis Battles (Grand Rapids: Baker, 1979), 55-9.

FREED TO SERVE THE WORLD

United to Christ, we come to share in Christ's victory. We are lords of all, says Luther. And yet, on the other hand, we are also dutiful servants of all.[44] 'In discussing this part of the subject Luther is at his very best as a religious teacher. The discussion is perhaps the finest thing he ever wrote,' says one commentator, 'the gem of Reformation literature.'[45] As another commentator puts it: 'Though justification by faith in Christ alone is central to the treatise, Luther balances the utterly passive nature of justification before God apart from works with the expectation of active responsibility on the part of the Christian living in the world for others.'[46]

The freedom of a Christian proclaimed by Luther is freedom to serve God and other people. Christians are not free in order to serve themselves. The modern myth is that we gain various freedoms in order to fulfil our desires. We loosen the chains of authority, so we can decide what is good and right and true and best for us. If God's idea of that is different from mine, then too bad for God – according to the gospel of modern Western culture. Yet Christian freedom is freedom to please God, not freedom to please myself. And this, crucially, is far better for society. As Michael Jensen has rightly said: 'Human freedom as conceived by Christian theology is superior to the hubristic secular version in

44. LW 31:344.

45. Mackinnon, *Luther and the Reformation*, 267. See also Luther's *Treatise on Good Works* in LW 44, from June 1520.

46. M. S. Whiting, *Luther in English: The Influence of His Theology of Law and Gospel on Early English Evangelicals (1525–35)*, (Eugene, OR: Pickwick Publications, 2010), 75.

that it recognizes the limits of creaturely existence and directs it to a purpose; and turns the subject away from self-advancement and towards the service of others. By comparison, the secular liberal myth of progressive human emancipation from authorities – such as and indeed especially God – produces outcomes that are problematic for human society.'[47]

So we return to the idea from the start of *The Freedom of a Christian*, where Luther says, 'It does not help the soul if the body is adorned with the sacred robes of priests or dwells in sacred places.' And 'it will not harm the soul if the body is clothed in secular dress, dwells in unconsecrated places.'[48] Christians can be kings and priests *in the world*, without having to hide away in monasteries, like St Benedict and others thought they had to do, to be faithful and pure. No 'Benedict Option' in that sense for Luther, and no strategy of hibernation. As Mackinnon puts it: 'He gives us a new ideal of the ordinary life in the world in opposition to the mediaeval, monastic view of separation from the world in the quest for individual salvation. The true sphere of the Christian is in the world, not apart from it.' So the 'consecrated individual life,' does not have to be lived 'in the cloister', but 'in the arena of the world'.[49] We can do all things to the glory of God, out in the mundane hustle and bustle of ordinary life.[50]

---

47. Michael Jensen, 'The Christian Revolution. 1: Liberty', *Churchman* 122 (2008), 154–5.

48. LW 31:345.

49. Mackinnon, *Luther and the Reformation*, 269-70.

50. Brad Gregory claims the Reformation had a complex and unintended influence which led to the secularisation of society, though what Luther

Luther also has another word for Christians who want to speak about these things to those around them. 'Whoever, therefore, does not wish to go astray with those blind men must look beyond works, and beyond laws and doctrines about works. Turning his eyes from works, he must look upon the person and ask how he is justified. For the person is justified and saved, not by works or laws, but by the word of God, that is, by the promise of his grace, and by faith.'[51] We don't have a list of works for people to complete. We have, in the gospel, a promise of freedom to proclaim.

So we are not just to go around telling all and sundry to repent, because they are sinners of one kind or another. They are sinners. They must fear God and repent of their sins. But we must not stop with that. Luther adds that 'we must also preach the word of grace and the promise of forgiveness by which faith is taught and aroused. Without this word of grace the works of the law, contrition, penitence, and all the rest are done and taught in vain.'[52] As Peter Stanford says in his biography of Luther as a Catholic dissident, all this 'was a powerful argument for grace, infused with a poetry that sits incongruously alongside Luther's use elsewhere of vulgar phrases.'[53]

What it means is that if we want to be Reformational Christians, we will not just be known as those who lay

---

seems to be trying to do here is not make everything secular, but make everything sacred. See Brad Gregory, *The Unintended Reformation: How a Religious Revolution Secularized Society* (London: Belknap Press, 2012).

51. LW 31:362-3.

52. LW 31:364.

53. Peter Stanford, *Martin Luther: Catholic Dissident* (London: Hodder and Stoughton, 2017), 212.

down the law and 'wag the finger' at the world around us because of how far it falls short of the law of God. We must be those who speak loudly and often about the word of grace and the promise of forgiveness. Only this can arouse faith and lead to changed lives and changed societies. As Vaughan Roberts rightly says, strident declarations of God's moral standards alone will not work – 'if we only respond to the iWorld and its promises of freedom and fulfilment with a list of laws, the best we can expect is nominal commitment – a half-hearted religious devotion that will eventually end in compromise. Laws will not capture people's hearts and transform their lives.'[54]

Shouting at the world not to rebel against God or live in ways that displease him, may feel good. We may feel that we are serving God's glory by flying his flag and defending his honour and 'criticising the unbelievers'. But our gracious God is most glorified when sinners repent and believe in his word – and when they are freed despite their works, despite their sin, by faith alone.

So let us not hide away from the world. And let us not scream at the world. But let us shine like stars in the universe, as we hold out the word of life – the gospel of true liberation – to a crooked and twisted generation; and live such good lives among the pagans, freely serving both them and the church, that they may glorify God on the day when he comes. As Luther himself prayed:

Merciful God, Heavenly Father, you have told us through the mouth of your dear Son, our Lord Jesus

---

54. Vaughan Roberts with Peter Jensen, *Faith in a Time of Crisis: Standing for the Truth in a Changing World* (Sydney: Matthias Media, 2017), 64.

Christ that, 'The harvest is plentiful, but the labourers are few; therefore pray earnestly to the Lord of the harvest to send out labourers into his harvest': In accordance with this, your divine command, we fervently pray that you would richly grant your Holy Spirit to all who are called to serve your word, that the multitude of your evangelists may be great, that we may stand faithful and firm against the world, the flesh, and the devil, and that your name may be hallowed, your kingdom grow, and your will be done.[55]

---

55. The final Collect in Luther's *Ordination of Ministers of the Word* (1539). See 'Barmherziger Gott, Himlischer Vater, Du hast durch den Mund' in *D. Martin Luthers Werke* (Weimarer Ausgabe), 38: 429-30 (third column, my translation).

JOHN CALVIN AND THE
REFORMATION MISSION

What does the Reformation have to do with mission? Aren't they two very different things? Reformation is about re-forming what is de-formed, rescuing something from obscurity, making it new again, purification. Whereas mission is about taking the gospel to new and exciting places where it has never been before. As Paul the great missionary once wrote: 'I make it my ambition to preach the gospel, not where Christ has already been named, lest I build on someone else's foundation, but as it is written, "Those who have never been told of him will see, and those who have never heard will understand"' (Rom. 15:20-21).

These two things are often seen as antithetical. So Stephen Neill in his classic *A History of Christian Missions* doesn't so much as mention Protestants in his chapter on sixteenth-century mission.[1] Later on, he simply adds a short note to say: 'In the Protestant world,

1. Stephen Neill and Owen Chadwick, *A History of Christian Missions* (London: Penguin, 1986), 120-50.

during the period of the Reformation, there was little time for thought of missions.'[2] Indeed, he concludes: 'when everything favourable has been said that can be said, and when all possible evidences from the writings of the Reformers have been collected, it all amounts to exceedingly little.'[3] He says everything that can be said about Protestants and mission in the sixteenth century is contained in just three pages of an obscure German work on the history of mission.

Cardinal Bellarmine (1542–1621), the great opponent of Protestantism, wrote a book on the fifteen marks of the true church in 1588. The ninth mark of a true church is that it has doctrine which converts souls. He says that 'heretics are never read to have converted any heathens or Jews to the faith, but only to have perverted Christians.'[4] They have only persuaded some people to go down the 'wide and easy road' which heretics open up for them. Whereas the true church 'drew the whole world … without arms and pomps … not to the delights of this world, but to things which must be believed beyond reason, and to the cross, the narrow and most perfect way … and all these things on account of no reward in this life, but only in the future life.'[5] He concludes:

---

2. Neill and Chadwick, *A History of Christian Missions*, 187.

3. Neill and Chadwick, *A History of Christian Missions*, 189, citing H. W. Gensichen, *Missionsgeschichte der neueren Zeit* (1961), 5-7.

4. Robert Bellarmine, *On the Marks of the Church* (Post Falls, ID: Mediatrix Press, 2015), 77 (chapter 12) translated from *De Controversiis Christianae Fidei Adversus Huius Temporis Haereticos: Tomus II, Liber IV, De Ecclesia* (Ingolstadt, 1588) by Ryan Grant.

5. Bellarmine, *On the Marks of the Church*, 78.

Lastly, in our own time many thousands of nations have converted to the Catholic faith. Some of the Jews also in individual years were converted and baptized at Rome by Catholics devoted to the Roman Pontiff, and even the Turks have not been lacking, who were converted both at Rome and at other places. On the other hand, the Lutherans have scarcely converted one or the other, although they compare themselves with the apostles and the evangelists.[6]

So the Reformation and true mission are two different things, it seems. The Roman Catholic Bishop of Geneva, Francis de Sales (1567–1622), claimed that Luther, Calvin, and other Protestants had no commission from God to preach and evangelize at all.[7] Others have since written of how the 'fundamental theological views' of the Reformers, 'hindered them from giving their activity, and even their thoughts, a missionary direction.'[8] According to one recent introduction to world missions, 'The Protestant Reformers … said little about foreign missions', because they believed that 'the world had been evangelised centuries before.'[9] Or as Timothy Tennent claims, 'The sixteenth century Protestant Reformation did not produce any missionaries.'[10]

6. Bellarmine, *On the Marks of the Church*, 80.

7. Francis de Sales, *The Catholic Controversy*, trans. H. B. Mackey (London: Burns and Oates, 1909), 11-32.

8. Gustav Warneck, *Outline of Protestant Missions from the Reformation to the Present Time*, trans & ed. George Robson (New York: Fleming H. Revell Company, 1901), 9.

9. A. S. Moreau, G. R. Corwin, and G. B. McGee, *Introducing World Missions: A Biblical, Historical, and Practical Survey* (Grand Rapids: Baker, 2004), 120-1.

10. T. C. Tennent, *Invitation to World Missions: A Trinitarian Missiology*

All of this rather paints the sixteenth-century Reformers and their heirs as stuffy, self-indulgent sticklers who cared more for their own ideological opinions and supposedly false theologies than for the salvation of lost souls, while Roman Catholicism seems to be the dynamic and enterprising engine of evangelism.

But none of this is entirely fair. For a start, as someone once put it, criticising the Reformers for not being engaged in world mission is a bit like criticising Columbus for not discovering Australia.

Consider the map of Europe at the time. Where are the great Protestant powers in the sixteenth century? They are in landlocked Switzerland, divided Germany, and in embattled England. The great Catholic missionary movements emanate from Spain and Portugal, which coincidentally happen to be the great maritime colonial powers of the day, with massive resources of manpower and gold committed to imperial expansion and control. Interestingly, we don't hear much of cross-cultural missionary endeavours from the Catholic powers of Poland or Hungary for example, or France – which did at least have access to the Atlantic. Once the Dutch and British broke out of Europe in the eighteenth century, they too did take the gospel with them, the Protestant gospel. So maybe there is more to it than simply 'Protestants are inward-looking and Catholics are not.' There is an element of opportunity and ability which must be taken into account here.

It is true that Protestants were often divided among themselves. They had their internal squabbles between

for the Twenty-First Century (Grand Rapids: Kregel, 2010), 248.

different kinds of Lutherans, between Lutherans and Reformed, and later between Reformed and Arminian. But this wasn't all that kept them from overseas mission, and Roman Catholicism has never been a totally united, monolithic institution either. There is also the fact that in many places during the sixteenth century, Protestants were fighting for their lives, often literally. Their freedom, their safety, and their very survival were precarious in that first century after Luther posted the 95 Theses. Nevertheless, the creation of vernacular Bibles and the preaching of reform did spread throughout the continent, from Iceland to Poland and beyond, even in that hostile environment.

The vast majority of the Protestant believers in Europe lived within easy striking distance of militarily powerful Catholic monarchs. Calvin's Geneva could easily have fallen to the King of France; on the other side of Switzerland, Ulrich Zwingli really did die in battle, defending Zurich from a vicious Catholic backlash; while Charles V was the most powerful man in Europe as both King of Spain and Holy Roman Emperor, and was a constant menace to most of the other Protestants on the Continent. There was much to be concerned about at home, in establishing the true profession of the gospel.[11]

---

11. For more on why intercontinental mission was not really feasible for early Protestants, see Kenneth Scott Latourette, *A History of the Expansion of Christianity* (London: Eyre and Spottiswoode, 1944), 3:25-30, and Glenn Sunshine, 'Protestant Missions in the Sixteenth Century' in Martin Klauber and Scott Manetsch (eds.), *The Great Commission: Evangelicals and the History of World Missions* (Nashville: B&H, 2008), 12-22, who counters the common argument that only the radical Anabaptists were interested in mission, not the magisterial Reformers.

On the other hand, we might examine Cardinal Bellarmine's audacious claim about the efficacy of Roman doctrine to convert people. We must all remember what the Lord Jesus said about how going great distances on mission is no guarantee that we are doing what pleases God: 'Woe to you, scribes and Pharisees, hypocrites! For you travel across sea and land to make a single proselyte, and when he becomes a proselyte, you make him twice as much a child of hell as yourselves' (Matt. 23:15). What kind of converts did Rome see in the sixteenth century as a result of the impressive journeys of Jesuit missionaries? Were thousands of people really converted, as Bellarmine said, 'without arms and pomps … not to the delights of this world … and all these things on account of no reward in this life, but only in the future life'?

That's not quite how it happened. In 1493, Pope Alexander VI (yes, the Borgia Pope who made his own illegitimate son into a cardinal) declared that the King of Spain could have lots of land on the other side of the Atlantic as long as he would also 'bring to Christian faith the peoples who inhabit these islands and the mainland … and to send to the said islands and to the mainland wise, upright, God-fearing, and virtuous men who will be capable of instructing the indigenous peoples in good morals and in the Catholic faith.'[12] The King of Portugal was allowed similar rights with similar duties, not only in the New World but also in India and the East. And what do we hear?

> In 1536, the entire caste of the Bharathas (Paravas), the fisherfolk of the Coromandel Coast, perhaps 10,000 of

---

12. Neill and Chadwick, *A History of Christian Missions*, 121.

them, was baptized. They had been suffering grievously from the depredations of Muslim raiders from the north. Poor, wholly illiterate, and helpless, they turned to the Portuguese for protection; protection was granted, the price to be paid for it being baptism. So all were baptized *en masse* – and then left for six years without instruction or pastoral care.[13]

Many converted precisely because of the force of arms, and the promises not of eternity but of the present. When Francis Xavier (1506–1552) came across these people some time later, he tried to instruct them, teaching them to say countless repetitions of paternosters and Ave Marias, and after the Lord's Prayer to cry out, 'Holy Mary, Mother of Jesus, obtain for us grace from thy Son, to enable us to keep the First Commandment.'[14] Neill also reports how the Philippines were 'after a fashion Christianized' in this way, but 'much of the Christianization remained very superficial' and the Jesuits there amassed vast riches which took up a lot of their time in administration. In Mexico it was the same: one of the Franciscan missionaries claimed: 'Often we baptized in a single day 14,000 people, sometimes 10,000, sometimes 8,000.'[15]

Big numbers were involved, but with what depth of faith? The Indian churches were almost entirely non-communicating throughout the century; that is, they were not permitted to participate in the Lord's Supper. They were also without indigenous leadership, and no

---

13. Neill and Chadwick, *A History of Christian Missions*, 127-8.

14. Neill and Chadwick, *A History of Christian Missions*, 128.

15. Neill and Chadwick, *A History of Christian Missions*, 143-4.

serious attempt was made to train and ordain native clergy.[16] All power was kept in the hands of the existing European hierarchy. No wonder Desiderius Erasmus (1466–1536), a Catholic himself, complained that the Roman Church's missionary efforts were neither deep nor heartfelt, did not adequately reflect the Church's resources, and could not be considered genuine if conducted at the point of a sword.[17]

With this kind of mission, you might be forgiven for thinking that the New World could have done with a little Reformation of its own. What the Reformation was, after all, was a movement 'to re-christianize Europe'.[18] There were serious and substantial vulnerabilities in the medieval church here, the greatest of which was the population's ignorance of the Christian message, despite the performance of repetitive rituals. Yes, they had sculpture and stained glass, a liturgical calendar, pilgrimages, and bishops. But the form of faith engendered was wide open to Protestant critiques. G. W. Bernard speaks in his recent study of the Late Medieval Church of 'an underlying pagan-cum-magical religious understanding upon which christianity [sic] had more or less been superimposed.'[19] That is, before

16. Neill and Chadwick, *A History of Christian Missions*, 148.

17. See his book on the art of preaching, *Ecclesiastes sive Concionator Evangelicus* (1535). Cf. Kenneth Stewart, *Ten Myths about Calvinism: Recovering the Breadth of the Reformed Tradition* (Nottingham: Apollos, 2011), 127-8.

18. Scott Hendrix, 'Rerooting the Faith: The Reformation as Re-Christianisation', *Church History* 69 (2000), 561.

19. Bernard, *The Late Medieval English Church*, 107. See also Scott Hendrix, *Recultivating the Vineyard: The Reformation Agendas of Christianization* (Louisville, KY: Westminster John Knox Press, 2004), 17.

the Reformation in Europe, there was a Christian sort of veneer over an essentially pagan religion, but no real grasp of the true nature of Christian faith as described in the Bible and practised in the early church.

So John Calvin was right, when, in 1555, he told the people of Geneva there were many 'false Christians who know less about God and his word than the natives of what we call the New Worlds.'[20] In the sixteenth century, Europe itself was a mission field. It would seem unfair to criticize those working and dying on one mission field for not also doing it on another at the same time.

Some may not have been as outward looking as they ought to have been. No doubt they could have used the opportunities for missionary evangelism presented by foreign refugees and immigrants into their own cities, for example, even if they could not travel across the seas to meet new races. Wolfgang Musculus (1497–1563), a Reformed professor of theology in Bern, complained to his compatriots: 'Alas, our depravity! Why do we not imitate the humanity of Christ? Why are we so inhumane toward foreigners and immigrants? Why do we not seize the opportunity for making known and extending the knowledge of Christ?'[21] Many did, however, look forward to and long for the worldwide spread of the true church. As Zwingli wrote: 'For the church refuses to be so narrowly restricted as to contain within it only a few members, and those few arrogating this honour to themselves alone; but, spreading over the whole world, it

---

20. John Calvin, *Sermons on Titus*, trans. Robert White (Edinburgh: Banner of Truth, 2015), 117-18.

21. Wolfgang Musculus, *Commentariorum in Evangelistam Ioannem: Heptas Prima* (Basel: Bartholomäus Westheimer, 1545), 45.

receives members everywhere; and the vaster and wider it is the more beautiful also is it.'[22]

THE WORD DID EVERYTHING

How did Luther and Calvin and Cranmer and others go about the Reformation, this re-Christianizing mission to Europe? We will look at Cranmer and the English Reformation later in this book. But let's think first about Luther in Saxony. In a sermon he once preached about love and law, Luther talks about the Roman Mass, and how it must be abolished as a sacrifice and a work of supposed merit.

> Yet Christian love [he says] should not employ harshness here nor force the matter … no one should be dragged away from it by the hair; for it should be left to God, and his word should be allowed to work alone, without our work or interference. Why? Because it is not in my power or hand to fashion the hearts of men as the potter moulds the clay and fashion them at my pleasure. I can get no farther than their ears; their hearts I cannot reach. And since I cannot pour faith into their hearts, I cannot, nor should I, force any one to have faith. That is God's work alone, who causes faith to live in the heart. Therefore we should give free course to the word and not add our works to it … We should preach the word, but the results must be left solely to God's good pleasure.[23]

We bring people to true faith not with harshness but with patient teaching of the word. When he says 'without our work or interference,' Luther doesn't mean to deny

---

22. Heller (ed.), *The Latin Works of Huldreich Zwingli: Volume 3*, 368.

23. LW 51:75-6.

a place to preaching or persuading or planning; what he means is clear: we don't argue for Christian things in un-Christian ways, by force or by cacophonous screeching. This had always been the way in the early church too, of course; Lactantius (250–325) wrote that 'there is no occasion for violence and injury, for religion cannot be imposed by force; the matter must be carried on by words rather than by blows, that the will may be affected.'[24] The Venerable Bede (673–735) made the same point when it came to the early evangelisation of England, insisting that 'the service of Christ must be accepted freely and not under compulsion.'[25]

Luther continued in his sermon on this subject, saying: 'We must first win the hearts of the people. But that is done when I teach only the word of God, preach the gospel … God would accomplish more with his word than if you and I were to merge all our power into one heap … For the word created heaven and earth and all things; the word must do this thing, and not we poor sinners … In short, I will preach it, teach it, write it, but I will constrain no man by force, for faith must come freely without compulsion.'[26] Thomas Cranmer said the same about trying to persuade his major theological opponent, Stephen Gardiner: 'Shall we perhaps … by severity and cruel behaviour overthrow him …? I do

---

24. Lactantius, *Divine Institutes*, 5:20. Mary Francis McDonald (trans.), *Lactantius: The Divine Institutes. Books I-VII* (Washington: Catholic University of America Press, 1964), 245.

25. *Ecclesiastical History*, I.26. Bede, *A History of the English Church and People*, trans. Leo Sherley-Price and R. E. Latham (London: Penguin, 1968), 71.

26. LW 51:76-7.

not take this to be the way to allure men to embrace the doctrine of the Gospel.'[27] Or as Richard Taverner preached: 'Infidels as Turks, Saracens, and Jews ought not violently to be drawn to our faith, but lovingly rather invited and allured.'[28]

Luther uses his own reformation in Wittenberg as an example of this. 'I opposed indulgences and all the papists,' he says, 'but never with force. I simply taught, preached, and wrote God's word; otherwise I did nothing. And while I slept [cf. Mark 4:26-29], or drank Wittenberg beer with my friends Philip and Amsdorf, the word so greatly weakened the papacy that no prince or emperor ever inflicted such losses upon it. I did nothing; the word did everything.'[29]

In this famous line, he is not encouraging idleness, contrasting the word with hard work. He is not promoting drunkenness. Still less is he saying that ministers should just turn up to preach on Sunday and do nothing more. He is contrasting word ministry with violence. His way was to preach, teach, and persuade people, not force them into faith, or to do massive hit-and-run baptisms.

But what if Luther had chosen some other way of achieving reformation? What if he had gone the way of harshness? He said: 'Had I desired to foment trouble, I could have brought great bloodshed upon Germany; indeed, I could have started such a game that even the

---

27. Null and Yates (eds.), *Reformation Anglicanism*, 64.

28. Richard Taverner, *The Epistles and Gospels with a Brief Postil upon the Same* (London, 1540), 42v.

29. LW 51:76-7.

emperor would not have been safe. But what would it have been? Mere fool's play. I did nothing; I let the word do its work.' Only one person is truly happy when the church tries to do things any other way. 'What do you suppose is Satan's thought when one tries to do the thing by kicking up a row?' asks Luther. 'He sits back in hell and thinks: Oh, what a fine game the poor fools are up to now! But when we spread the word alone and let it alone do the work, that distresses him. For it is almighty, and takes captive the hearts, and when the hearts are captured the work will fall of itself.'[30]

So it is incumbent upon us, he says, 'in the midst of an even desperate situation to see it through gently and bring everything to an orderly conclusion.'[31] It is God's work, not ours, which reaches into the soul and changes minds. Only God working through his word can actually transform people's hearts. Which is why Luther translated the Bible into a language people could understand, preached that word constantly, wrote commentaries on it, and trained others to go and do the same. His activity served his strategy, while the Jesuit missionaries did what served theirs: they baptized *en masse* but did not always instruct, kept people away from the Supper, and did not focus on training others *in situ*, but on retaining control and amassing wealth. These missionary strategies are different, and they win people to different forms of faith.

---

30. See The Second Sermon, 10 March 1522, Monday after Invocavit in LW 51:75-8 (WA 10[III], 18-19).

31. LW 17:216.

The Question on which Everything Hinges

One further thing should be noticed, about Reformation doctrine. It was not simply being picky about indulgences and the power of the Pope. There was a more basic issue involved. I mentioned before the debate Luther had in print with the humanist Reformer Erasmus on the issue of free will and salvation. Luther said this was 'the question on which everything hinges'.[32] The vital question was this: are we saved eternally by grace alone, or not? That is the defining issue of the Reformation, and it is a missiological question. The Reformation was ultimately a matter not of money, or of power, or of culture, or of politics – but of eternal salvation.

Erasmus said that Luther's whole idea of salvation *sola gratia*, by grace alone, undercut evangelism. Luther said that by nature we do not have free will, and therefore all we can do (on our own) is sin. So if we are to be saved, it must be by grace alone. That was too extreme for Erasmus. Erasmus countered that we must have free will, to choose God, so it was not all by grace alone. We need some grace, but we add it to our free choice, and by doing so we are saved.

Erasmus defined free will as 'a power of the human will by which a man can apply himself to the things which lead to eternal salvation, or turn away from them.'[33] This ability to choose salvation is damaged by sin, but not extinguished by it.[34] So we can present the

---

32. LW 33:294.

33. Erasmus, *On the Freedom of the Will* in E. Gordon Rupp and Philip S. Watson (trans. and eds.), *Luther and Erasmus: Free Will and Salvation* (Philadelphia: Westminster Press, 1969), 47.

34. Erasmus, *Freedom of the Will*, 51.

gospel to people and call on them to repent, because they can, if they want to. But Luther's whole idea of 'our will is enslaved to sin, so salvation is all by grace alone' makes evangelism pointless, he said. Why evangelise, why go on mission to the pagans at all, if they are unable to choose to follow Jesus, that is, to join the striving of their will to the assistance of divine grace? As he says: 'What is the point of so many admonitions, so many precepts, so many threats, so many exhortations, so many expostulations, if of ourselves we do nothing, but God in accordance with his immutable will does everything in us, both to will and to perform the same?'[35]

Luther, however, would not give up the idea of preaching the life-giving word of God to everyone, just because we are by nature unable to respond to it without God's help. Rather, like Ezekiel preaching to the valley of dry bones in Ezekiel chapter 37, he simply obeyed the command to preach, and trusted God to do his work in people by his Spirit as he did so.[36] So as Charles Chaney concludes: 'Thus, while Luther held tenaciously to the doctrine of God's sovereign choice in the election of his people, this in no way hindered him from proclaiming the Gospel of forgiveness to all men.'[37] For Luther, the gospel was to be unconfined, and 'will be diffused over all parts of the world,'[38] – 'neither shall his praise, his worship, and his people

---

35. Erasmus, *Freedom of the Will*, 87.

36. There is more on Luther's argument against Erasmus in my *Cornerstones of Salvation*, 15-42.

37. Charles Chaney, 'Martin Luther and The Mission of the Church' in *Journal of the Evangelical Theological Society* 13.1 (Winter 1970), 23.

38. LW 13:10.

be limited but shall extend to all the kingdoms of the earth.'[39]

ELECTION AND EVANGELISM

If this accusation – that Reformation doctrine undercuts mission – was thrown at Luther, you can imagine it was also thrown at John Calvin, who is nowadays known most of all for teaching the doctrine of predestination or election. What is the point of mission and evangelism if God has already decided in eternity who will be saved?

Luther was quite confident that the whole world would come one day to hear the gospel. As he comments on 'Praise the Lord all you heathen!' in Psalm 117: 'Wherever there are heathen – or a country or a city – there the Gospel will penetrate and will convert some to the kingdom of Christ.'[40] Calvin also longed for that to happen. It is a gross misunderstanding of his doctrine of predestination to think that it implies a lack of interest in the conversion of the world to Christ.[41]

In his book on predestination, Calvin says: 'Since we do not know who belongs to the number of the predestined and who does not, it befits us to feel as to wish that all be saved. So it will come about that, whoever we come across, we shall study to make him a sharer of peace.'[42] This is a natural desire for any true Christian.

39. LW 13:34.

40. LW 14:13.

41. See J. I. Packer, *Evangelism and the Sovereignty of God* (Leicester: IVP, 1961).

42. John Calvin, *Concerning the Eternal Predestination of God*, trans. J. K. S. Reid (Louisville, KY: Westminster John Knox Press, 1997), 138.

As he comments on Isaiah 2:3, 'Come let us go up to the mountain of the LORD':

> By these words he first declares that the godly will be filled with such an ardent desire to spread the doctrines of religion, that every one, not satisfied with his own calling and his personal knowledge, will desire to draw others along with him. And indeed nothing could be more inconsistent with the nature of faith than that deadness which would lead a man to disregard his brethren, and to keep the light of knowledge choked up within his own breast. The greater the eminence above others which any man has received from his calling so much the more diligently ought he to labor to enlighten others.[43]

Calvin also preached in one of his sermons on Deuteronomy that, 'When we know God to be our Father, should we not desire that he be known as such by all? And if we do not have this passion, that all creatures do him homage, is it not a sign that his glory means little to us?'[44] The missionary urge is natural for all who truly know God. So we pray and wish the best for all peoples. First Timothy 2:1 implies that we are to pray explicitly for foreign nations, 'for all people'. God wishes that the gospel should be proclaimed to all without exception, preaches Calvin, so 'we must not only pray for the faithful, who are our brethren already,

---

43. John Calvin, *Commentary on the Book of the Prophet Isaiah: Volume First*, trans. William Pringle (Grand Rapids: Baker, 1993), 94.

44. *Ioannis Calvini Opera quae supersunt omnia* 29, edited by G. Baum, E. Cunitz, and E. Reuss (Brunswick: C. A. Schwetschke, 1885), 175, translated in Michael A. G. Haykin and C. Jeffrey Robinson Sr., *To the Ends of the Earth: Calvin's Missional Vision and Legacy* (Wheaton, IL: Crossway, 2014), 61.

but for those who are far off, such as poor unbelievers. Although there seems to be a great distance and a thick wall between us, yet we must nevertheless have pity on their destruction and pray to God that he would draw them to himself.'[45] We do not know whether it will please God to have mercy on them or not, but we ought to hope well, since they are made in the image of God. Even if they are on the road to damnation, our salvation from that was only by the free goodness of God, and so theirs might be too.[46]

In the transcripts of Calvin's sermons, we often have at the end a note of how he prayed when he had finished preaching. With alarming regularity, for those who think he did not care about such things, Calvin prayed that God's grace would extend 'not only to us but also to all peoples and nations of the earth.'[47] Prayer for world mission was a regular part of Genevan liturgy.[48] So as Michael Haykin and Jeffrey Robinson say: 'Calvin thus held firmly to the doctrine of predestination with one hand while clinging to the continuing validity of the Great Commission in the other. He did so because the Bible seems to do the same.'[49] This is why the Synod of

---

45. John Calvin, *Sermons sur La Première Epitre à Timothée in Ioannis Calvini Opera 53*, 128 (my translation).

46. *Ioannis Calvini Opera* 53:135.

47. John Calvin, *Sermons on the Epistle to the Ephesians*, trans. A. Golding (Edinburgh: Banner of Truth, 1973), 475; cf. pages 21, 49, 126, 184, 241, 505, 591. See also Haykin and Robinson, *To the Ends of the Earth*, 56.

48. See Elsie McKee, 'Calvin and Praying for "All People Who Dwell on Earth"', *Interpretation: A Journal of Bible and Theology* 63.2 (April 2009), 130-40.

49. Haykin and Robinson, *To the Ends of the Earth*, 46.

Dort, summarising Calvinist teaching at the start of the seventeenth century, would joyfully proclaim:

> The promise of the gospel is that whoever believes in Christ crucified shall not perish, but have eternal life. This promise ought to be declared and published promiscuously and without distinction, to all nations and people to whom God according to his good pleasure sends the gospel, together with the command to repent and believe.[50]

This double commitment, to predestination in theology and to promiscuously evangelistic fervour and prayer, was not merely a theoretical exercise for Calvin. As Bruce Gordon tells the story: 'Beginning in 1555 Geneva began its most audacious missionary effort in France by sending ministers to serve in the nascent Protestant churches.'[51] Geneva in those days was only about the size of Buxton, Chesham, or Crowborough in the U.K., with a population of approximately 21,000 people. There are around 2,000 cities bigger than that in the U.S.A. today. And yet Calvin's Geneva managed between 1555 and 1562 to send over 100 Protestant missionaries into the Roman Catholic heartlands of France. In 1555, there were only five Reformed churches in the whole of that kingdom. Just seven years later, in 1562, it is estimated that there were around 2,000 Reformed churches planted in France.

---

50. Canons of Dort, 2:5. See Lee Gatiss, *For Us and For Our Salvation: 'Limited Atonement' in the Bible, Doctrine, History, and Ministry* (London: Latimer Trust, 2012), 81. There is more on missiology in the Calvinist confessional tradition in Wes Bredenhof, *To Win Our Neighbors for Christ: The Missiology of the Three Forms of Unity* (Grand Rapids: Reformation Heritage Books, 2015).

51. Bruce Gordon, *Calvin* (London: Yale University Press, 2009), 312.

In Rouen, about 20 per cent of the city became Protestant Christians. About half of the upper and middle class converted, so that there were around two million Protestant Christians.[52] Calvin himself was involved in every aspect of this effort, though he himself did not set foot back in his home country. Gordon says 'the growth of the Reformed churches in France was nothing short of spectacular', as the Vaud (the canton around Geneva) was itself stripped of clergy to serve this missionary effort.[53] This is astonishing. Especially for a little city with a relatively new church led by a man whose doctrine supposedly made him anti-mission and anti-evangelism.

The French connections also enabled Geneva to send missionaries to Brazil.[54] From Geneva to Brazil hardly seems like a natural development! The Lord High Admiral of France just happened to be a Huguenot, a French Protestant. So when France was planning to start a colony out in Brazil (near Rio), the leader of the expedition asked Geneva to send him some ministers and well instructed Christian artisans to go with the 600 colonists. This they joyfully did.[55] It did not go very well, as it turns out. They planned to stay and were working

52. See Haykin and Robinson, *To the Ends of the Earth*, 69.

53. Gordon, *Calvin*, 315.

54. There is a fascinating account of the journey by one of the participants in Jean de Léry, *History of a Voyage to the Land of Brazil*, trans. Janet Whatley (Berkeley, CA: University of California Press, 1990).

55. De Léry, *History of a Voyage*, 4-5: 'When the Church of Geneva received his letters and heard his news, it first rendered thanks to God for the extension of the realm of Christ into so distant a country, even into so strange a land, and among a nation that was indeed completely ignorant of the true God.'

on long-term strategies to develop bilingual translators,[56] but the leader of the expedition turned against the missionaries when they were out there. Though they could perhaps have resisted him, it was well known that they went there 'to live according to the reformation of the Gospel'. So, wrote one of them, 'fearing to stain the latter, and wanting to leave him no occasion to complain of us, we preferred to obey.'[57] They were therefore exiled away from the colony and had to wait for months to get a ship home.[58] But those plucky Genevans grabbed the opportunity, the open door, when it was offered to them, and gave it a shot on a foreign mission field.[59]

Philip Hughes, my esteemed predecessor as Director of Church Society, was therefore right when he painted a picture of Protestant Geneva as more of a shipyard than a school, more a missionary centre than a Protestant ghetto:

> Human vessels were refitted in this haven, not to be status symbols like painted yachts safely moored at a fashionable marina, but that they might launch out into the surrounding ocean of the world's need, bravely facing every storm and peril that awaited them in order to bring the light of Christ's gospel to those who

---

56. See R. Pierce Beaver, 'The Genevan Mission to Brazil' in John Bratt (ed.), *The Heritage of John Calvin* (Grand Rapids: Eerdmans, 1973), 62.

57. De Léry, *History of a Voyage*, 49-50.

58. See Amy Glassner Gordon, 'The First Protestant Missionary Effort: Why Did it Fail?', *International Bulletin of Missionary Research* 8.1 (January 1984), 12-18.

59. See Haykin and Robinson, *To the Ends of the Earth*, 71. Cf. G. Baez-Camargo, 'The Earliest Protestant Missionary Venture in Latin America', in *Church History* 21 (1952), 135-45.

were in the ignorance and darkness from which they themselves had originally come ... Geneva became a dynamic center or nucleus from which the vital missionary energy it generated radiated out into the world beyond.[60]

The motto of Geneva is *Post tenebras lux*. Calvin's Geneva sought, diligently, to bring light to the darkness.

CONCLUSION

So we see that the Protestant Reformation was itself a movement to re-Christianize a pagan, superstitious Europe. While Catholic powers were engaged in mass baptisms in the New World, the Reformers had their attentions mostly fixed on the Indians at home in their own churches and their own nations.[61] They were not ignorant of the challenge of world mission, and they longed for the gospel to be heard by all. They played their part in the Great Commission by living and dying for the faith right here in Europe – translating and preaching the word and sowing the seeds for a movement of world mission which would in time expand, with the Protestant empires of England and Holland in the coming centuries.

---

60. Philip E. Hughes, 'John Calvin: Director of Missions' in John H. Bratt (ed.), *The Heritage of John Calvin* (Grand Rapids: Eerdmans, 1973), 44-5.

61. In his short tract, *The Hirelings Ministry* (published in London in 1652), Roger Williams, the controversial founder of Providence (Rhode Island), highlighted the ongoing importance of domestic mission in the seventeenth century. There are not just Indians in America, he said, but, 'We have Indians at home, Indians in Cornwall, Indians in Wales, Indians in Ireland ... who can deny but that the body of this and of all other Protestant Nations (as well as Popish) are unconverted?' See my 'The Puritans as Missionaries' in *Modern Reformation* 20.2 (March-April 2011), 7-9.

To conclude then, far from being mutually exclusive, reformation and mission are intimately linked. They are in fact simply the contextual outworking of the gospel in different circumstances. When you regain the gospel, you soon discover a need to retell it to others. May we also be passionate to engage in reform-mission, for the glory of God and the good of our world, today. Let us pray, as Calvin did in his church liturgy:

> We offer up our prayers unto thee, O most gracious God and merciful Father, for all men in general, that as thou art pleased to be acknowledged the Saviour of the whole human race, by the redemption accomplished by Jesus Christ thy Son, so those who are still strangers to the knowledge of him, and immersed in darkness, and held captive by ignorance and error, may, by thy Holy Spirit shining upon them, and by thy gospel sounding in their ears, be brought back to the right way of salvation, which consists in knowing thee the true God and Jesus Christ whom thou has sent.[62]

---

62. John Calvin, 'Forms of Prayer for the Church' in Henry Beveridge (ed.), *John Calvin: Tracts and Letters. Volume 2: Tracts, Part 2* (Edinburgh: Banner of Truth, 2009), 102.

Thomas Cranmer and the
Evangelistic Strategy of the
Prayer Book

During the Reformation, there were Reformation Anglicans interested in world mission. One such was Hadrian Saravia (1532–1613), the evangelist of Jersey and Guernsey and later a prebendary of Westminster Abbey.[1] Despite his own Dutch background, Saravia was also one of the translators of the King James Version of the Bible. In his *Treatise on the Different Degrees of the Christian Priesthood* (1590), he writes:

> The command to preach the Gospel and the mission to all nations were so given to the Apostles, that they must be understood to be binding on the Church also. The injunction to preach the Gospel to all nations of unbelievers had respect not only to the age of the Apostles, but to all ages to come till the end of the world … Christ commanded his Church to provide that the Gospel should be preached to unbelievers, after the departure of the Apostles, according as

---

1. See Michael Nazir-Ali, *From Everywhere to Everywhere: A World View of Christian Mission* (Eugene, OR: Wipf and Stock, 1991), 43-4.

opportunities of time, place, and persons should admit.[2]

Saravia wondered whether the lack of world mission in his day was due to 'a lack of persons fit to be sent' or 'a lack of zeal for the extension of Christ's kingdom'.[3] Either way, he was making this point because he thought it important for the church to commit this Great Commission to suitable people as opportunities arose. One place where the opportunity certainly did arise, however, was in England itself.

Ashley Null and John W. Yates III write that: 'Outreach has been a part of the DNA of Christianity in Great Britain from its first introduction during Roman times. Heirs to this legacy, the English Reformers believed that Christ had come to proclaim a message that had the power to gather a community. As a result, the church's number one task was to call people to repentance and new life in Jesus Christ. Everything about the church – its structure, worship, preaching, pastoral care, and outreach into the community – had to be designed to support this mission directive.'[4] So in this chapter we will be exploring how Archbishop Thomas Cranmer and the first generation of Reformers tried to reach their own nation for Christ, particularly by means of the *Book of Common Prayer*. How did that beautiful piece of liturgical brilliance serve the mission directive and attempt to fulfil the Great Commission?

---

2. Hadrian Saravia, *A Treatise on the Different Degrees of the Christian Priesthood* (Oxford: John Henry Parker, 1840), 161-2.

3. Saravia, *Treatise*, 164-5.

4. Null and Yates (eds.), *Reformation Anglicanism*, 192-3.

Many people find liturgiology (the study of church liturgy) a little bit boring: the endless comparisons between different editions of the Prayer Book, weighed against modern versions, addressing the minutiae of phraseology and seemingly nit-picking objections to instructional rubrics. Just finding one's way around the different books and knowing where we are in the liturgical calendar can be somewhat taxing, not to mention the lectionaries, the method for calculating the date of Easter, the moveable feasts, and the directions telling you what to do with your hands, when to kneel, and so on.

I am aware that all this brings a delicious thrill to the spine for certain people, and there is a growing interest in Reformation liturgy even amongst younger evangelicals.[5] But for others it can seem a little dull. Liturgy is lifeless. It is a dead letter, and they want the dynamism of worship in a different and more modern style, unencumbered by the rigid moulds and forms of a bygone era. These people may appreciate some aspects of the *Book of Common Prayer* (BCP) – its doctrine, its magnificent language – but it does not particularly warm their hearts or guide the ways they think about church on a Sunday. Surely we want to worship God with our hearts, not just our liturgical lips (Matt. 15:8-9)? And isn't it all a bit 'Anglican' or 'Episcopalian' or even Roman Catholic?

There are many things we can all appreciate about the *Book of Common Prayer*, which should unite Bible-

---

5. See the excellent new compilation of sixteenth-century liturgies in Jonathan Gibson and Mark Earngey (eds.), *Reformation Worship: Liturgies from the Past for the Present* (Greensboro, NC: New Growth Press, 2018).

loving, gospel-hearted Christians of various stripes and backgrounds. Above all else, however, I think the BCP was an evangelistic tool. That, I think, is its real heartbeat. The *Book of Common Prayer* is evangelism, tailored specifically to the Anglican mission in England. This fantastic piece of precise liturgical genius was a key part of the Protestant Reformers' evangelistic strategy to reach the nation for Christ. Its intent was to proclaim to the people of England what the Queen's Coronation oath calls, 'the true profession of the gospel … the Protestant Reformed religion', which Reformed evangelicals such as me so dearly love and rely on.[6]

So in this final chapter, let's examine the idea that the Prayer Book was at least partly a tool for mission. Though let me say up front: it wasn't *just* about evangelism. The BCP is a prayer book, a service book, a book to aid us in our worship of the one true and living God. It is, as Brian Cummings reminds us, 'a book to live, love, and die to' – for baptisms, weddings, and funerals.[7] It is a book designed to fill us with awe and reverence as we participate in its rituals and regularities, rather than an evangelistic tract to be read out to a congregation every Sunday.

But still, the Prayer Book has a mission edge. It is carefully put together to teach the gospel, and to reach people's hearts with the message of salvation. Its much praised eloquence is all in the service of an impassioned plea to trust, obey, and please the Lord Jesus who died

---

6. See Lee Gatiss, *The True Profession of the Gospel: Augustus Toplady and Reclaiming our Reformed Foundations* (London: Latimer Trust, 2010).

7. Brian Cummings, *The Book of Common Prayer: The Texts of 1549, 1559, and 1662* (Oxford: OUP, 2011), xii.

for his family, the church.[8] Because, as William Whitaker (1548–1595) said, defending the vernacular liturgy, 'nothing can be more dignified, majestic, or holy than the Gospel.'[9] So this is not a stuffy old book for stuffy old people. What we are considering here is classic, confessional evangelism, which Reformed Christians of all stripes can cherish and be inspired by, and which stands as a great reminder of what Reformation evangelism could look like.

I want to unpack this idea of the evangelistic Prayer Book by looking at what the BCP teaches us in three particular areas. What does it communicate about the Bible? What does it say about the cross and salvation? And how does it encourage us to live as believers? After thinking about its approach to the Bible, the cross, and Christian living, we will finish by considering how the Prayer Book, even after 350 years, could still be useful and instructive for *our* evangelism today.

THE PRAYER BOOK AND THE BIBLE

Let's start with what the Prayer Book communicates to its users about the Bible.

To start with, it is worth remembering that there is actual doctrinal content in the Prayer Book.[10] The *Thirty-nine Articles* were deliberately bound up together

---

8. See the first Collect for Good Friday where Christ is said to have died for 'this thy family'.

9. William Whitaker, *A Disputation on Holy Scripture, Against the Papists, especially Bellarmine and Stapleton* (Cambridge: Cambridge University Press, 1849), 251.

10. See John Richardson, 'Have we an Anchor? Reasserting the Doctrinal Role of the Book of Common Prayer' in *Faith and Worship* 68 (2011).

with the orders of service in the BCP, so that people could see the doctrinal basis and confessional statement of the national church. I think this is one way in which *Common Worship* (the Church of England's more modern liturgy) has let Anglicans down. The Articles of Religion are strikingly absent from the books which make up *Common Worship* – and the excuse cannot be given that there is insufficient space, because *Common Worship* takes up several volumes and is all available electronically too.

What do the Articles and the rest of the Prayer Book say about the Bible? Two or three years ago I remember watching a televised debate about some contentious issues within the church. It doesn't matter what it was. A bishop was on (it doesn't matter which one) and as part of his contribution he signalled that what Scripture says cannot be taken as the word of God. During the debate, a Lay representative on General Synod (a member of my church at the time) had quoted a passage of Scripture which directly addressed the issue being discussed. Yet the bishop refused to countenance this, saying instead that, 'For Christians "the word of God" is the life of Jesus. The Bible is the product of those who sought to understand the life of Jesus.' It was a subtle and clever way to avoid the clear teaching of the verses that had been quoted, what the Puritans might have called an evasive tergiversation.

The bishop thus drove a wedge between Christ and his word, as many others have also done. It should be pointed out clearly and immediately that this is not the official teaching of the Church of England, which everywhere acknowledges that the Bible is the word of

God. It is to be treated and obeyed as such, whether the human author of any particular passage is Moses, Peter, or Paul. Since that is in much doubt today, particularly on the big issues in church life, this truth perhaps requires a short demonstration.

The Anglican formularies are emphatic that God is the author of Scripture and that the Bible – not just Christ – is his word. This could be illustrated from text after text after text, but a few examples from various portions of the official formularies like the Prayer Book ought to suffice to prove the point. The Canons of the Church of England, its legal code, state that 'The doctrine of the Church of England' whilst being 'grounded in the Holy Scriptures' is 'to be found in The *Thirty-nine Articles of Religion*, the *Book of Common Prayer*, and the Ordinal' (Canon A5). Hence I have chosen texts from each of these documents to show what official Anglican teaching, derived from the Reformation, actually is.

The Canons themselves refer to the Bible as 'God's word' in Canons A2, A3, A4, and A6. They speak of things being 'not repugnant to the word of God', and in Canon A5 of things being 'agreeable to the said Scriptures'. Article 20 of The *Thirty-nine Articles* even refers to the Bible as 'God's Word Written'.

The preface 'Concerning the Service of the Church' in the *Book of Common Prayer* speaks of 'the very pure word of God, the Holy Scriptures', and ministers are encouraged to read and meditate upon 'God's word' (which clearly cannot refer here to Christ, since he cannot be 'read'!). The order for the Visitation of the Sick in the BCP contains these words: 'God, who hast written thy holy word for our learning …' The Bible is

God's holy word *written*. That view is written in to BCP services. Such language is also found in several Collects (short prayers).[11]

In the BCP Communion Service the minister prays, 'We are taught by thy holy word, that the hearts of Kings are in thy rule' (cf. Prov. 21:1). They affirm that it is God 'who by thy holy Apostle hast taught us to make prayers … for all men' (1 Tim. 2). Thus the Bible is seen as God's word, through which he teaches his people, even now, though the human authorship of the Scripture is also acknowledged. The Litany prays that God will 'illuminate all Bishops, priests, and deacons, with true knowledge and understanding of thy word; and that both by their preaching and living they may set it forth.' (Note: 'set it forth' rather than 'set *him* forth' which is what one would expect if it was Christ being spoken of as the word, rather than the Bible.)

In the Ordinal – the services used to ordain new ministers – the congregation pray, 'that we may have grace to hear and receive what they [the newly ordained presbyters] shall deliver out of *thy most holy word*, or agreeable to the same, as the means of our salvation' [my italics]. The ministers themselves are exhorted to 'drive away all erroneous and strange doctrines contrary to *God's word*.' We might wish that this were indeed happening more frequently, but it is a key part of what an authentic Anglican minister is supposed to do.

During the Reformation, Thomas Cranmer and other Reformers produced *The Homilies of the Church*

---

11. See those for Advent 2, St Peter's Day, and St Andrew's Day for example.

of England. These are official sermons referred to in Article 35 as containing 'godly and wholesome Doctrine' which is useful for congregations to hear. One of the homilies is appropriately titled, 'An Information for them which take offence at certain places of the Holy Scripture.' There it says that the Scriptures were 'written by the inspiration of the Holy Ghost' and are 'the word of the living God', even 'his infallible word'.[12] Reformation Anglican doctrine is that the Bible is infallible.[13] There is even a case to be made for an authentically Anglican doctrine not only of infallibility but even of the inerrancy of the Bible. Article 21 reminds us, for example, that alongside erring and errant General Councils, the holy Scripture itself is alone to be considered as finally trustworthy, as it cannot lead us astray.[14]

Thomas Cranmer, the prime architect of the English Reformation, revered Scripture as 'God's own words'.[15] We might also quote Richard Hooker (1554–1600), a supposedly quintessential Anglican, who was equally clear that the Bible itself is the word of God.[16] But even

---

12. John Jewel, *The Second Tome of Homilees* (London, 1571), 294-315.

13. See Richard Hooker, *Of the Laws of Ecclesiastical Polity: Volume 2. Book V*, trans. Arthur Stephen McGrade (Oxford: OUP, 2013), 13, (V.i.4) where he speaks of 'true and infallible principles delivered unto us in the word of God as the axioms of our religion.'

14. See Lee Gatiss, 'The Unerring Word of God' in *The Gospel Magazine* 2674 (September-October 2010), 152-4, and *The True Profession of the Gospel: Augustus Toplady and Reclaiming our Reformed Foundations* (London: Latimer Trust, 2010), 56.

15. Thomas Cranmer, *Works* (edited by J. E. Cox; Cambridge: Cambridge University Press, 1844–1846), vol. 2, 106 (lxxi).

16. e.g., Hooker, *Laws of Ecclesiastical Polity: Volume 2. Book V*, 56 (V.xxi.2) and 66 (V.xxii.10) where he says, 'Wherefore when we read or

further back, St Augustine stated that what the Bible says, God says,[17] thus indicating that this is in fact the historic, classic, orthodox Christian position to take on Scripture. It has its origins in Scripture itself of course, e.g. Hebrews 1:1 'God spoke ... through the Prophets', and 2 Timothy 3:16 'All Scripture is God-breathed'. Ultimately, as Christians (disciples of Christ) we acknowledge the Bible as our authority simply because that is what Christ himself did. The definitive answer in debate for him was always 'Have you not *read* what *God said*?' (e.g. Matthew 22:31, see also 12:3, 5; 19:4).[18]

So then, when Scripture is read out in meetings, committed Anglicans need have no qualms of theological conscience as they liturgically affirm 'This is the word of the Lord'. It is only the agenda of certain theologians and lobbyists which has caused some to doubt or deny this. Although those supposedly 'modernizing' impulses have sadly gained ground in recent years, loyal members of the Church of England who know the doctrine of the Prayer Book should not lose their confidence in the Bible as the very word of the living God.

So that is the message which comes across propositionally in the *Book of Common Prayer* and elsewhere in the Church of England's formularies. The Bible is the unerring word of God himself. It is the source and summit of authority in the Church according to the Prayer Book, a revelation from Almighty God himself

recite the scripture, we then deliver to the people properly the word of God.'

17. *Confessions*, xiii.29.

18. See Lee Gatiss, 'Biblical Authority in Recent Evangelical Books' in *Churchman* 120.4 (2006), 321-35.

that is worthy of our careful and special attention. As John Stott said: 'Scripture is the sceptre by which King Jesus reigns.'[19]

Is this relevant for mission? We should, naturally, acknowledge that the Prayer Book was written in different times. In those days people were perhaps more likely to be asking 'How can I know God and be saved?' than they are today. And the Prayer Book directs them to the Bible as the place to find the answer. Today, the question people on the streets are more likely to be asking is, 'Is there really a God, and how can I know?' But again, the Prayer Book is pointing them to the source of the answer. It claims time and time again that the Bible is a word from God. Is there a God? Yes, he is there and he has spoken. How can I know? Because we have that word, and you can see and read it for yourself. As Jim Packer put it: 'God's purpose in revelation is to *make friends* with us', and we have that revelation in his word.[20]

Now, some people tend to learn things propositionally like that. They can look through the book or hear it each week and pick out specific propositions to take away. Others, as we know, will learn things more by osmosis. So what do we pick up about the Bible by osmosis, so to speak, from the Prayer Book of the English Reformation?

---

19. John Stott, *Evangelical Truth: A Personal Plea for Unity* (Leicester: IVP, 1999), 67. The image of Scripture as Christ's 'sceptre' may originate with John Calvin, e.g., *Institutes* 3.20.42; 4.2.4.

20. J. I. Packer, *God Has Spoken* (London: Hodder and Stoughton, 1993), 50. As Packer also says (page 52), to say that divine revelation is non-propositional is actually to de-personalize it; modern theology too often gives us 'a Lover-God who makes no declarations!'

One of the prayers which churchgoing people would hear most often was the so-called 'Prayer for the Church Militant' in the Communion service. Three times in this prayer the foundational role of the word of God in our life together is reiterated. The minister asks God to, 'grant, that all they that do confess thy holy Name may agree *in the truth of thy holy word*, and live in unity, and godly love.' Next, the congregation asks God to 'Give grace, O heavenly Father, to all Bishops and Curates, that they may both by their life and doctrine *set forth thy true and lively word*, and rightly and duly administer thy holy Sacraments.' Finally, what is it they pray for themselves, even before they pray for those who are sick or in any kind of need? 'And to all thy people give thy heavenly grace; and specially to this congregation here present; that, with meek heart and due reverence, *they may hear, and receive thy holy word*; truly serving thee in holiness and righteousness all the days of their life.' The repetition is striking and was designed to make an impact.[21]

This is why the Prayer Book prescribed a healthy and robust diet of Bible reading and preaching for every church. Again, as Packer rightly says, 'The Anglicanism of the 1662 Prayer Book, with its hundred-verses-a-day lectionary, its monthly passage through the Psalter, its Bible-crammed daily services, and its high valuation of expository preaching … is a Bible-reading, Bible-loving, Bible-believing faith.'[22] If one followed all the set readings

---

21. I'm very grateful to my friend Christopher Idle for particularly pointing out these references to me.

22. Packer, *God Has Spoken*, 119-20. Sadly, he goes on, 'Today, however, Anglicans devote their zeal to maintaining a state of doctrinal laxity rather than a confession of biblical truth.' Some Anglicans, that is, not all!

laid down in the BCP, one would get through the Bible at a fairly rapid pace. This exceeds the expectations of every other church, whether in Rome, Wittenberg, or Geneva. So during the Reformation, the English church became the Bible-hearing church *par excellence*, because Cranmer wanted all people, not just the chosen few locked away in monasteries, to be able to ruminate and meditate on Scripture and for it to change their hearts and everyday lives.[23]

Moreover, let us not forget, this was all happening *in English*. What a revolution that was, to have the word of God in the language people understood. And of course, the BCP is also in a language people understood. It wasn't necessarily the language of the street or the farm. It was not meant to be. But it was English, and it was intended to communicate something. Many modern liturgies are actually founded on the principle of 'studied ambiguity'[24] – they deliberately obfuscate in order to gloss over doctrinal issues, piling up high sounding rhetoric without actually saying *anything* coherent or intelligible, often quite deliberately to create a sense of confusion and so-called 'mystery'. But the BCP is saying,

---

23. See Null and Yates (eds.), *Reformation Anglicanism*, 71, 76. James Packer, 'For Truth, Unity, and Hope: Revaluing the Book of Common Prayer' in *Churchman* 114.2 (2000), 105 says 'it is plain that our Reformers meant the Anglican Church to become the greatest Bible-reading church in Christendom, and Anglican Christians to become the most knowledgeable Bible students to be found anywhere.'

24. For 'studied ambiguity' in liturgical use see *An Order for Holy Communion* (London: SPCK, 1966), viii; R. T. Beckwith & J. E. Tiller (eds), *The Service of Holy Communion and its Revision* (Abingdon: Marcham Manor Press, 1972. Latimer Monograph III), 28; and R. C. D. Jasper & Paul E. Bradshaw, *A Companion to the Alternative Service Book* (London: SPCK, 1986), 172.

we can know God. We English-speaking people can hear his word and grasp it. We can respond in kind, in English, and be heard.

So while it retains a sense of dignity, and does not forget God's transcendent holiness, the BCP communicated to those taking part in its services that God is near to each one of us. And it urged them to call upon him, while he is near, from their hearts, in their own language.

So that's my first point, on the Bible as God's word written. The BCP was designed, as Cranmer said, so that 'the people (by daily hearing of holy Scripture read in the Church) might continually profit more and more in the knowledge of God, and be the more inflamed with the love of his true Religion.'[25]

SALVATION SECURED FOR SINNERS

The next thing I want to look at is what the Prayer Book teaches us about salvation. Remember, I am saying that the BCP was designed to be an evangelistic tool, part of a strategy to convert England to the biblical, Reformed faith. It is not just a grand liturgical monument. So what does it say about salvation?

The Reformers Cranmer, Ridley, and Latimer all died as martyrs because they refused to submit to the Roman Catholic doctrine of the Mass. So-called transubstantiation, the changing of the substance of the bread and wine in the Lord's Supper into the body and blood of Christ himself was the great dividing issue. The English Reformers refused to believe this, teach

---

25. From 'Concerning the Service of the Church', one of the prefaces to the *Book of Common Prayer*.

this, or to countenance the superstitious practices that had grown up around it, because they did not find such doctrine in the Scriptures. Royal injunctions fulminated against 'works devised by men's fantasies … [such] as wandering to pilgrimages, offering of money, candles, or tapers to relics or images, or kissing and licking of the same, praying upon beads, or such like superstition … for that they be things tending to idolatry and superstition.'[26] And in every case, it was their opposition to transubstantiation and all that accompanies it, which led to their execution. They literally went to the stake and were burned for their view of the Lord's Supper.

These people were not ritualists. They were not merely concerned with the ceremonial niceties of the Lord's Supper. What concerned them was the wrong view of Christ and salvation which was put forward by the Roman rite and by various superstitious practices. They were teaching people error, leading them astray, away from salvation. But what did they put in the place of the Mass? What was it that they taught Reformation Anglicans to pray and to remember as they gather around the Lord's table?

They taught in the English Prayer Book that the Supper is a divine instrument of assurance. We are urged to confess our sins to God – our 'manifold sins and wickedness'. We are miserable offenders, pitiable. We are unworthy sinners. Our biggest and most pressing problem is not psychological or economic. Our problem is that God is angry with our sin and we need to be

---

26. See Gerald Bray, *Documents of the English Reformation* (Cambridge: James Clarke & Co., 1994), 248 (cf. 176, 181, 255).

forgiven for it. So as Article 2 puts it, Christ came 'to reconcile his Father to us'. And in the Communion service we are assured by the words of Scripture itself that 'Christ Jesus came into the world to save sinners' (1 Tim. 1:15) and that 'he is the propitiation for our sins' (1 John 2:2). We come to the table, 'not trusting in our own righteousness, but in God's manifold and great mercies'.

So worshippers come with nothing in their hands to receive God's mercy. This is not the medieval idea of 'God will not deny grace to those who do what is in them.'[27] It is not 'God helps those who help themselves and do a little for God.' Emphatically, no. In the Prayer Book, salvation is all about God doing something, not us. The movement of the action in this liturgy is from God to us: God in his grace reaching down to us in our sinfulness, to help. We simply take and eat in remembrance of what he has done. The Protestant missionary strategy was, as Ashley Null puts it, 'to allure their people back to God with the good news of Jesus's genuine, gentle concern for humanity's own inner longings.'[28]

So the whole Communion service is a divine instrument of assurance. Its intention is to show us that although we are more wicked than we ever thought, we are also more loved by a merciful God than we ever dreamed. The result is that pastorally speaking our consciences are assured of God's love towards us

---

27. Cf. Heiko A. Oberman, '*Facientibus quod in se est Deus non denegat Gratiam*: Robert Holcot, O.P. and the Beginnings of Luther's Theology' in *Harvard Theological Review*, 55.4 (October 1962), 317-42.

28. Null and Yates (eds.), *Reformation Anglicanism*, 122.

even when we've been most searingly honest about our shortcomings and failures. The Prayer Book directs us to the one place where forgiveness and peace can be found – in the cross of our Lord Jesus Christ. Anglicans praise God, in one of their post-Communion prayers, 'that by the merits and death of thy son Jesus Christ, and through faith in his blood, we and all thy whole Church may obtain remission of our sins, and all other benefits of his Passion.'

There are other ways of arranging a Communion service, and other ways of phrasing the prayers to give a different message altogether. We could give the impression that something magical happens at a particular moment in the service and that we can appropriate that magic somehow. We could give the impression to God that we are doing something for him, offering him something, going through a ritual for his benefit. But that would be to turn the Lord's Supper into a duty, another work we're meant to do; whereas Cranmer was concerned to make the liturgy preach the gospel of grace from beginning to end.

Cranmer makes it very clear that what is going on at the Lord's *table* is not a sacrifice on an altar made by a mediating priest on behalf of the people which has to be repeated again and again each week to be effective. That was the message people got from the Mass. In the Mass, something is offered to God. According to the Council of Trent (which authoritatively declared the Roman view), the Mass is 'truly propitiatory', for 'appeased by this sacrifice, the Lord grants the grace and gift of penitence and pardons the gravest crimes and sins.' Indeed, anyone who thinks a true and real propitiatory sacrifice is not offered to God in the Mass is anathematized by

113

the Tridentine Canons.[29] Instead, what Cranmer has ministers say, as they lead the Anglican service, is that Christ's once-and-for-all sacrifice on the cross on our behalf was utterly, completely, and totally sufficient to pay for all our sins. No additional sacrifice, no other manner of offering, is necessary.[30]

So look at the opening of the prayer of consecration, and the repeated emphasis here:

> Almighty God, our heavenly father, which of thy tender mercy didst give thine only son Jesus Christ, to suffer death upon the cross for our redemption, who made **there** [not *here* on the table!] (by his **one** oblation of himself **once** offered) a **full**, **perfect** and **sufficient sacrifice**, **oblation**, and **satisfaction**, for the sins of the whole world, and did institute, and in his holy Gospel command us to continue, a perpetual **memory** of that his precious death, until his coming again.

Cranmer does like to bang home his point doesn't he? So there is no sense in which what is happening at the *table* is a sacrifice. All the language of us making a sacrifice is kept until after we've eaten. Only then do we pray that God would accept, to use the language of Hebrews 13, a sacrifice of praise and thanksgiving. So after we've fed

29. See *The Canons and Decrees of the Council of Trent*, translated and edited by H. J. Schroeder (Rockford, IL: Tan Books, 1978), 149 (22nd Session; 17 September 1562, chapters 2 and 9). See also *Catechism of the Catholic Church* (London: Geoffrey Chapman, 1999), 304-7 (§1350, §1357, §1365).

30. *Catechism of the Catholic Church*, 307 (§1367) claims that 'The sacrifice of Christ and the sacrifice of the Eucharist are *one single sacrifice*' (emphasis original), but that 'only the manner of offering is different.' He who offered himself in a bloody manner is now supposedly offered in an unbloody manner by others.

on Christ in our hearts by faith, we offer and present to God not the bread and wine but ourselves, to use the language of Romans 12, as a holy and lively (or living) sacrifice.

So in the Church of England's official and much-beloved liturgy, we have assurance of sins forgiven through faith alone in the work of Christ alone, which is utterly sufficient for all. To a people brought up on medieval Roman Catholicism, this was a powerful and very deliberate proclamation of the biblical gospel of grace alone.

The basic – covenantal – structure of the Prayer Book Communion service is a threefold repetition of a simple gospel theme: we acknowledge our sin, hear the grace of the gospel, and respond to it in faith. So first we pray the Collect for purity and pray for mercy for having broken God's law; then we hear the New Testament readings; then we say 'I believe' (in the creed), hear the sermon, give to the collection, and pray in faith. The second time round, we pray the confession; then we hear the absolution and words of comfort and forgiveness; and finally we respond in thanksgiving and praise to the Lord Most High. The service then repeats this cycle a third time: we again confess our unworthiness to come to the Lord's Table trusting in our own righteousness, in the prayer of humble access; then the grace of God in sending Jesus to die as a sufficient sacrifice in our place is proclaimed in the prayer of consecration; and finally we respond again by feeding on Christ in our hearts by faith as we take and eat the bread and wine, then pray and sing our thanksgiving. Guilt, grace, and the gratitude of faith are three times inculcated in those who use this service by this deceptively straightforward reiteration of the gospel and celebration of the work of Christ on the cross.[31]

Nowadays, I have to say, many Communion liturgies try to do too much. They are so packed out with different themes and a profusion of perspectives (in order to accommodate the variety of theologies now held in our churches) that they don't have a simple and clear message. It's almost the case that sometimes they don't rivet our attention on the cross *at all*. Worshippers can be left at best confused and bewildered, or at worst deeply in error, about the supper and the gospel it is meant to proclaim. Outsiders have no idea what's going on and draw all kinds of strange and inappropriate conclusions, not just from the words of our liturgies but from the choreography and costumes and distracting stage-props.

The language of sacrifice is often moved from where Cranmer put it, *after* we have eaten and drunk, to *before* – which can give a totally different impression of what is going on. See, for example, Eucharistic Prayer A in *Common Worship* which includes the line 'Accept through him, our great high priest, this our sacrifice of thanks and praise, and as we eat and drink these holy gifts …' This takes the sacrificial offering language from where Cranmer had placed it (after the eating and drinking, as part of the thanksgiving after receiving) and strongly associates it instead with what is happening on the table at that point in the service.[32] Oftentimes,

31. I owe the observation of the three cycles to J. I. Packer's booklet, *The Gospel in the Prayer Book* (1966).

32. *Common Worship* (London: Church House Publishing, 2000), 187; cf. Prayer C (p. 193) which does the same. The error can be

the collection is now presented immediately before the eucharistic prayer, so that as Andrew Atherstone has put it, 'Before gathering around the Lord's Table to be reminded of God's grace, we are first asked to open our wallets!'[33] The Communion service in the original Prayer Book was, in contrast to this, a terrific evangelistic tool. It enabled believers to focus on Christ and his work on our behalf to 'redeem our souls from the jaws of death'.[34]

Modern people often seem to think that God would be fortunate to have their worship and service. He should be pleased that they so graciously deign to cross the threshold of the church every few weeks. He needs the business, doesn't he? They might perhaps consider going to him for some comfort or inspiration – or to track down a Pokémon character – or if there's no sport on TV or parties for the kids. But it often seems never to cross their minds that they *need* the forgiveness for which Christ shed his blood, or that it could be theirs by faith alone.

Cranmer's Prayer Book service is a reminder from the Reformation that we are all sinners in need of salvation, which Christ alone can offer. We are in danger of forgetting that message, if we obscure it with medieval and Roman innovations – or if we rush through our Communion services just for the sake of it once a quarter or so – without remembering what Cranmer was trying to pass on to us, sealed with his own blood.

---

compounded by gestures towards the elements as the minister says 'this our sacrifice'.

33. Andrew Atherstone, 'The Lord's Supper and the Gospel of Salvation' in Lee Gatiss (ed.), *Feed My Sheep: The Anglican Ministry of Word and Sacrament* (London: Lost Coin, 2016), 82-3.

34. See the Thanksgiving for Deliverance from Plague in the BCP.

THE CHRISTIAN LIFE

So we've looked at what the BCP tells us about the Bible, a revealed and written word from the speaking, living God. And we've looked at what it communicates to us about the depths of our sin and salvation *sola fide*. As one of the Collects put it, 'We put not our trust in any thing that we do.'[35] Now, more briefly, let us look at what it says about the Christian life, because the *evangel* itself is also a call to discipleship and the Great Commission includes teaching people to obey all that Christ has commanded (Matt. 28:20). The purpose of this book is to remind us how the Reformers regained, retold, *and relied on* the gospel of grace.

Again, the Christian life is a life dependent on God's grace, according to the BCP. I think we see that very clearly in some of the Collects, for example. So the Collect for Trinity 19 says, 'O God, forasmuch as without thee we are not able to please thee; mercifully grant, that thy Holy Spirit may in all things direct and rule our hearts, through Jesus Christ our Lord, Amen.' Note the Augustinian, Reformed emphasis on being unable to please God without God's own help. Romans 8 teaches us that of course – verse 8 'Those who are in the flesh cannot please God.' Or Philippians 2, God works in us 'to will and to work for his good pleasure'. Or Hebrews 13, he must work in us 'that which is pleasing in his sight'. But it is also there in the Articles: 'we have no power to do good works pleasant and acceptable to God without the grace of Christ preventing us [going before us], that we may

---

35. The Collect for Sexagesima.

have a good will, and working with us when we have that good will' (Article 10).

Original sin remains even in those who are regenerate according to Article 9, and according to the rest of the Prayer Book too. In one of the Advent prayers we are meant to confess that 'through our sins and wickedness, we are sore let and hindered in running the race that is set before us.' So, in turn, Cranmer has people pray that 'thy bountiful grace and mercy may speedily help and deliver us.' Help us run the race, by your grace.

Prayer Book users pray on Christmas Day that they 'may daily be renewed by thy Holy Spirit'. The Collect for Innocents' Day asks God to 'mortify and kill all vices in us, and so strengthen us by thy grace, that by the innocency of our lives and constancy of our faith, even unto death, we may glorify thy holy name.' Kill our vices, by your grace.

I could pile up examples of how the Prayer Book, and particularly the Collects, speaks of our need for grace in running the Christian life. How it is a life empowered by the Holy Spirit, by which we put to death our vices. This is unimpeachably Reformational doctrine turned into prayer. It reminds us of an important truth that many today have forgotten: Jesus does not meet all my felt needs; many of them he mortifies.

All Anglican ministers promise at ordination to proclaim *this* inheritance of faith afresh in their generation.[36] How can anyone do that unless they know what faith we have inherited? What is the Reformational way to live? This Prayer Book will tell us – it's about

36. See Canon C15 Of the Declaration of Assent.

leaning on God's grace to mortify our sins and live for others to God's glory. Part of that will even mean praying for 'Jews, Turks, Infidels, and Heretics' to be fetched home to Christ and saved,[37] because Cranmer cared not just for little England, but for the salvation of the world.

James Devereux has shown how Cranmer sometimes used pre-existing Latin Collects with a distinctly Augustinian voice, and sometimes gave others a distinctly Reformed twist.[38] All along he was trying to teach that we need God's special grace to go before us to put good desires into our minds, and his continual help to bring those desires to good effect, as we reach out with the gospel of grace to others.

In the Communion service, the people recite the Ten Commandments and plead for mercy – since we have all broken them. And they ask God to 'incline our hearts to keep this law.'[39] But the Collects also sum this up: '… because through the weakness of our mortal nature we can do no good thing without thee, grant us the help of thy grace, that in keeping of thy commandments we may please thee both in will and deed' says one; while another pleads for 'such a measure of thy grace that we, running the way of thy commandments, may obtain thy gracious promises.'[40]

---

37. See the Collect for Good Friday.

38. James A. Devereux, 'Reformed Doctrine in the Collects of the First Book of Common Prayer' in *Harvard Theological Review* 58.1 (1965).

39. This is the Reformed view of the Law in devotional form. See Lee Gatiss and Peter Adam, *Reformed Foundations, Reforming Future: A Vision for 21st Century Anglicans* (London: Lost Coin, 2013), 20.

40. See the Collects for Trinity 1 and Trinity 11.

So we see that the Prayer Book counters both the Pelagian tendency and the Antinomian tendency. That is, it neither overstresses good works nor overplays grace, but keeps them both in their correct gospel places. The so-called 'Anglican way', if the Prayer Book is any guide, is consistent Reformed theology in prayer and practice, neither lawless, nor legalistic. This is the grace-driven Christian life for which we are saved and to which the gospel of Christ calls us. As the Swiss Reformed scholar, Samuel Leuenberger, says:

> How timeless in its relevance and important in its message is a liturgical prayer book which, with revivalistic power, maintains the everlasting truths of Scripture in their true position amidst life's daily storms. The *Book of Common Prayer* which has illuminated Christian worship in England for the last five centuries, is just such a liturgy.[41]

IS THIS USEFUL TODAY?

So is this doctrinal and liturgical heritage useful for today? And am I encouraging everyone, Anglican or otherwise, to use *Book of Common Prayer* services in our churches every Sunday, as my prescription for modern evangelism? Let me be clear: no, I am not.

Just as the church in Jeremiah's day was not safe simply because they trusted in 'the temple of the Lord, the temple of the Lord, the temple of the Lord' (Jer. 7:4), neither will twenty-first-century Anglicans reach the lost or 'reform and renew' their churches simply by

---

41. Samuel Leuenberger, 'Archbishop Cranmer's Immortal Bequest: The Book of Common Prayer of the Church of England: An Evangelistic Liturgy' in *Churchman* 106.1 (1992), 31.

chanting, 'The Articles of Religion, the Book of Common Prayer, the Ordinal and Homilies!' That would be romantic antiquarianism. Neither Confessional Baptists, Presbyterians, nor Anglicans are helped by adopting such an inerrantist stance towards their founding documents, however solid they may be. Such formularies must be believed and obeyed (inasmuch as they point us to Christ), and translated into a language 'understanded of the people' (Article 24), not just tenaciously held on to like prize exhibits in a museum.

That said, 1662 services can be very good, and still have their place.[42] I learned a lot by taking BCP Communion services regularly during my first few years as an Anglican minister, and not just at 8 a.m. with a dedicated handful either; sometimes at 11 a.m. as well, with full-robed choir and Anglican plainchant Psalms. The Prayer Book is still usable today, even in younger congregations, with perhaps just a little updating, provided such variations are 'reverent and seemly and shall be neither contrary to, nor indicative of any departure from, the doctrine of the Church of England in any essential matter.'[43]

Other denominations are unlikely to take up such a practice. Besides, we all have to admit that the BCP was an evangelistic tool for a liturgical people. It was

---

42. The 1662 edition of the Prayer Book is now the authoritative one in the Church of England, though it is essentially the same doctrinally as the books drafted during the Reformation under Thomas Cranmer in 1549 and 1552, and re-authorised for use by Elizabeth I in 1559.

43. Canon B5. If all Anglicans do is translate the Prayer Book into a modern idiom, in obedience to Article 24, then that seems to me to be perfectly legitimate. More than that, it is beneficial and edifying.

designed to teach people who were used to church and liturgy a more Reformed and Protestant way to pray and worship God. It was a strategy which made a huge amount of sense in a time and culture where most people went to church every Sunday and holy day. Its majestic language passionately pleaded with people to engage their hearts in serving a merciful God, who sent his Son to save wretched sinners by faith alone. It expounded that gospel and urged congregations to respond.

Now, I assume that we too want to passionately plead with people to engage their hearts in serving a merciful God, who sent his Son to save wretched sinners by faith alone. The reading and preaching of the Scriptures must be at the heart of that evangelistic effort. That's what the Prayer Book assumes: that people are converted by the Spirit of God through the word of God – and it prescribes serious doses of the word, not just a verse or two followed by a jokey 'talk' with PowerPoint slides and balloons. Are we courageous enough to follow that same course, even if we don't use the same sixteenth- and seventeenth-century language in our prayers before the sermon? We should be reading more than a few verses each Sunday. As Richard Hooker says:

> With us there is never any time bestowed in divine service without the reading of a great part of the holy scripture. Which we account a thing most necessary. We dare not admit any such form of liturgy as either appoints no scripture at all or very little to be read in the Church. And therefore the thrusting of the bible out of the house of God is rather there to be feared, where men esteem it a matter so indifferent whether the same be by solemn appointment read publicly or

not read, the bare text excepted which the preacher haply chooses to expound.[44]

The fashion in many churches, both high and low, whether Anglican or not, seems to be to spend more time singing or listening to music than attending on God's word read and preached. If the words of our songs and anthems are scriptural, the damage may be mitigated, but not entirely avoided. This was a problem identified during the Reformation by those who put together the English Prayer Book. Peter Martyr Vermigli, for example, Italian-born Regius Professor of Divinity at Oxford and one of the architects of the 1549 and 1552 Prayer Books, was concerned that our choral traditions would undermine the ministry of the word and lead us back in a Roman direction. 'Almost everywhere in the papal religion they think they have worshipped God sufficiently in the Church when they have sung and shouted loud and long,' he declared. 'There are many priests and monks who think they deserve well of God because they have sung many psalms.'

Vermigli identified this vice as an issue to be addressed because 'there should not be so much singing in church as to leave almost no time for preaching the word of God and holy doctrine.' And yet, he said, 'We can see this happening everywhere in a way, for everything is so noisy with chanting and piping [or strumming and drumming?] that there is no time left for preaching. So it happens that people depart from church full of music and harmony, yet they are fasting and starving for heavenly doctrine.' He added this challenge:

---

44. Hooker, *Laws of Ecclesiastical Polity: Volume 2. Book V*, 50 (V.xx.5).

[Some early churches] used either very little singing or almost none at all. They saw the people's weakness to be such that they paid more attention to the harmony than to the words. So today if we see Christians running to church as to the theater, where they can be amused with rhythm and singing, in such a case we should abstain from something not necessary, rather than feed their pleasures with the destruction of their souls.[45]

This is perhaps sage advice for churches which find themselves in a culture of entertainment. Vermigli says that if people literally are amusing themselves to spiritual death, pushing out preaching by a fixation on 'good music'; if what they are really interested in deep down is a good morning or evening out for a 'performance' or singalong at church (or chapel or cathedral) – then, rather than pandering to it and trying to imitate the world's musical idioms, we should stop singing in church altogether. We should not baptize the latest musical trends and hope to win a hearing for the gospel through good quality Christian music in our meetings; but stop it altogether, to expose the sinfulness and deception at work in such desires, and point people to a better way. We need to be feeding our souls with the word, to the destruction of the flesh, rather than feeding our pleasures with music, to the destruction of our souls.[46]

---

45. Vermigli, *De Musica et Carminibus* from *In Librum Iudicum* (Zurich: Froschauer, 1561), chapter 5, fols. 73r-74v as translated by J. C. McLelland in J. P. Donnelly, F. James, and J. C. McLelland (eds.), *The Peter Martyr Reader* (Kirksville, Missouri: Truman State University Press, 1999), 171-2.

46. Notwithstanding the clear injunction in Ephesians 5:19 and Colossians 3:16 for us to speak to one another and to our own hearts by means of psalms, hymns, and spiritual songs, of course!

Liturgy itself seems to be rather out of favour at the moment.[47] That may be for various reasons. For example, in the UK over the last few generations, many church leaders in so-called 'influential churches' became Christians *despite* their exposure to liturgical worship (often in private school chapels), rather than because of it. So over many years they have often sought to escape what they consider to be less edifying liturgical constraints in favour of a meeting structure more reminiscent of a Christian summer camp, since that is where they often first experienced conversion and authentic discipleship. Liturgy may also be considered spiritually distasteful by those in nonconformist traditions, because of a lingering communal memory of how the Prayer Book was heavy-handedly imposed by the 1662 Act of Uniformity.[48] Luther wrote – quite rightly – about how liturgy ought not to 'entangle anyone's conscience' and be rigidly insisted on.[49] So, as Andrew Atherstone concludes: 'The spiritual health of a liturgy is to be measured not only by its doctrinal and devotional content, but also by the manner in which it is enacted. The words on the page may declare the gospel of grace, but if imposed in a legalistic manner (perhaps by a later generation),

---

47. See the admonitory article by the Cambridge Baptist pastor, Julian Hardyman, 'The Curious Death of Evangelical Liturgical Worship?' in *Crossway* 130 (Autumn 2013), 3.

48. See my *The Tragedy of 1662: The Ejection and Persecution of the Puritans* (London: Latimer Trust, 2007).

49. LW 53:61. This was also the burden of John Owen's *A Discourse concerning Liturgies, and their Imposition* (1662).

that grace is contradicted.'[50] This may be why liturgy *per se* is denigrated in some circles.

The danger is that because of these understandable background influences, many evangelicals may have thrown out the baby with the bathwater. Does it hinder our evangelism to pray the Lord's Prayer, or recite the great truths of the gospel in the creeds, or prayerfully remind ourselves of the Ten Commandments? And yet we think singing a batch of worship songs with a live band may help to reach the un-evangelised fringe with the gospel? They may have their place, but might it not also help to strengthen our congregations and save us a good deal of time and effort in catechesis, if we were more careful in constructing our Sunday services along the covenantal lines that the Reformers did? Moreover, as Andrew Atherstone also warns: 'Liturgical invention, *de novo*, is inherently sectarian. A blank sheet of paper frequently results in departure from apostolic patterns and thus divides the Church.'[51]

In some churches I've been in, even evangelical churches, there is no public confession of sin. That was introduced by Cranmer in an effort to do away with compulsory auricular confession to a priest, which the Fourth Lateran Council had imposed on all and Trent endorsed with its usual dismal anathemas.[52] Without a

---

50. Andrew Atherstone, 'Reforming Worship: Lessons from Luther and Cranmer' in *Churchman* 132.2 (2018), 108.

51. Atherstone, 'Reforming Worship', 121.

52. See Canon 21 of the 1215 Lateran Council, and Canon 6 of the 14th Session of the Council of Trent. In the first exhortation before Communion in the Prayer Book (from 1552 onwards), the Minister does say that 'if there be any of you, who by this means cannot quiet his own conscience herein,

proper public confession, we may slip back into that – except maybe we will call it Christian counselling with our pastor or 'spiritual direction', which will become more and more the desired norm both in and out of the pulpit. We don't want to alienate visitors; but is it not more dangerous still to give the impression that we are no longer wretched sinners in need of forgiveness, but victims in need of affirmation and therapy?

In some churches I've been in, even evangelical churches, there is no regular rendition of the creeds. That was intended to remind us week by week of the great central truths of our Trinitarian faith and the facts surrounding Christ's death 'for us and for our salvation'. Without it, we may need to put on special courses – even for church members – to teach them anew what every regular churchgoer in 1662 (and for a hundred years before that) would have recited habitually and known instinctively. How does it help either our discipleship or our evangelism to be so neglectful?

In some churches I've been in, even evangelical churches, there is no use of carefully composed Collects. We really do just prefer the less disciplined and less thoughtful ramblings of the untrained and unsupervised laity in public intercessions, because this is somehow more 'authentic'. Yet does it also lead to casual Patripassianism,

---

but requireth further comfort or counsel, let him come to me, or to some other discreet and learned Minister of God's word, and open his grief; that by the ministry of God's holy word he may receive the benefit of absolution, together with ghostly counsel and advice, to the quieting of his conscience, and avoiding of all scruple and doubt.' But this is not mandatory for all, and nor does it speak of a sacrament of penance or (like 1549 and before) of secret, auricular confession to a priest; rather, we have a general confession, and the ministry of God's word by a learned minister.

Arianism, Pelagianism, Antinomianism, and all kinds of other heresies, as we push out the balanced biblical and Trinitarian diet of Reformation worship? It is this, let it not be forgotten, which made it instinctively difficult for the Church of England to go Unitarian, as so many of the non-liturgical, non-creedal 'free churches' did, in the century after 1662. As Catherine LaCugna has rightly affirmed: 'The liturgy far more than theology kept alive in Christian consciousness the trinitarian structure of Christian faith.'[53]

In some churches I've been in, even evangelical churches, there is no saying or praying through the Ten Commandments. And consequently, even many evangelical ministers couldn't now tell you what all Ten Commandments are or in what order they appear in the Bible. Our theological education may give us seemingly erudite thoughts about cultural apologetics, postmodern hermeneutics, or the complexities of gender theology. But are we clueless about the basics, such that the average sixteenth-century churchgoer would put us to shame? How does it help our evangelism if we sideline God's law? Indeed, it is interesting to note that people often learned to read during the Reformation using catechisms: they picked up their ABCs precisely in order to read the Ten Commandments, the Creed, and the Lord's Prayer, which were also often plastered on the

---

53. Catherine LaCugna, *God For Us* (San Francisco: HarperCollins, 1991), 210. See also H. J. MacLachlan, *Socinianism in Seventeenth Century England* (Oxford: Oxford University Press, 1951), 334, and Philip Dixon, *Nice and Hot Disputes: The Doctrine of the Trinity in the Seventeenth Century* (London: T&T Clark, 2003), 215-16, who says that 'The sheer rhythm of the Liturgy familiarized churchgoers with belief in the Trinity.'

walls of their churches in English. But how well known are those crucial texts today?

In some churches I've been in, even evangelical churches, they have never even thought about how to proclaim afresh in this generation the Reformed faith, such as is found in The *Thirty-nine Articles* and the *Book of Common Prayer*, along with other Reformed confessions and liturgies. May that not be true of those who read these pages. Let us not venerate these historical helps or use them slavishly. But let us not neglect what Cranmer and others died to give us.

Many of the doctrinal and ethical and evangelistic mountains we face today would be substantially easier to climb if we had not abandoned this precious inheritance over the course of the last fifty years. And, as I hope I have also demonstrated, there is ripe evangelistic fruit to be reaped here as well. As the great evangelical preacher, Charles Simeon of Cambridge, once wrote: 'At the commencement of the Reformation the most lamentable ignorance prevailed throughout the land ... If then the pious and venerable Reformers of our Church had not provided a suitable form of prayer, the people would still in many thousands of parishes have remained in utter darkness; but by the diffusion of this sacred light throughout the land, every part of the kingdom became in good measure irradiated with scriptural knowledge, and with saving truth.'[54]

May there be more such light in the darkness of our own days. So we conclude with 'A Collect or Prayer

---

54. From Simeon's sermons on the Liturgy (1812); see Andrew Atherstone, *Charles Simeon on the Excellency of the Liturgy* (Alcuin Club/GROW Joint Liturgical Study), 72; Norwich: Hymns Ancient and Modern, 2011, 23.

for all Conditions of men' from the *Book of Common Prayer*, where we pray for all people, and especially for the universal church:

> O GOD, the Creator and Preserver of all mankind, we humbly beseech thee for all sorts and conditions of men; that thou wouldest be pleased to make thy ways known unto them, thy saving health unto all nations. More especially we pray for the good estate of the Catholick Church; that it may be so guided and governed by thy good Spirit, that all who profess and call themselves Christians may be led into the way of truth, and hold the faith in unity of spirit, in the bond of peace, and in righteousness of life ... And this we beg for Jesus Christ's sake.

Collects and Prayers

Lord, God Almighty, who by your Spirit has united us into your one body in the unity of the faith, and has commanded your body to give praise and thanks unto you for that bounty and kindness with which you have delivered your only begotten Son, our Lord Jesus Christ unto death for our sins: grant that we may fulfil this your command in such faith that we may not by any false pretences offend or provoke you who are the infallible truth. Grant also that we may live purely, as becomes your body, your sons and your family, that even the unbelieving may learn to recognize your name and your glory. Keep us, Lord, lest your name and glory come into ill repute through the depravity of our lives.

Ulrich Zwingli

Almighty God, the protector of all who hope in you, without whose grace no one is able to do anything, or to stand before you: Grant us your mercy in abundance, that by your holy inspiration we may think what is right, and through your power perform the same; for the sake of Jesus Christ our Lord.

Martin Luther

Lord, give to your people grace to hear and keep your word that, after the example of your servant William Tyndale, we may not only profess your gospel but also be ready to suffer and die for it, to the honour of your name; through Jesus Christ your Son our Lord, who is alive and reigns with you, in the unity of the Holy Spirit, one God, now and for ever.

Modern Anglican Collect for 6 October

Merciful God, Heavenly Father, you have told us through the mouth of your dear Son, our Lord Jesus Christ that, 'The harvest is plentiful, but the labourers are few; therefore pray earnestly to the Lord of the harvest to send out labourers into his harvest': In accordance with this, your divine command, we fervently pray that you would richly grant your Holy Spirit to all who are called to serve your word, that the multitude of your evangelists may be great, that we may stand faithful and firm against the world, the flesh, and the devil, and that your name may be hallowed, your kingdom grow, and your will be done.

Martin Luther

We offer up our prayers unto thee, O most gracious God and merciful Father, for all men in general, that as thou art pleased to be acknowledged the Saviour of the whole human race, by the redemption accomplished by Jesus Christ thy Son, so those who are still strangers to the knowledge of him, and immersed in darkness, and held captive by ignorance and error, may, by thy Holy Spirit shining upon them, and by thy gospel sounding in their ears, be brought back to the right way of salvation, which consists in knowing thee the true God and Jesus Christ whom thou has sent.

John Calvin

O GOD, the Creator and Preserver of all mankind, we humbly beseech thee for all sorts and conditions of men; that thou wouldest be pleased to make thy ways known unto them, thy saving health unto all nations. More especially we pray for the good estate of the Catholick Church; that it may be so guided and governed by thy good Spirit, that all who profess and call themselves Christians may be led into the way of truth, and hold the faith in unity of spirit, in the bond of peace, and in righteousness of life ... And this we beg for Jesus Christ's sake.

Prayer for all Conditions of Mankind,
from the *Book of Common Prayer*

CHRISTOPHER CATHERWOOD

FIVE LEADING REFORMERS

Lives at a watershed of history

MARTIN LUTHER
THOMAS CRANMER
JOHN CALVIN
JOHN KNOX
ULRICH ZWINGLI

"Each in his way was a watershed figure, and Catherwood's vivid profiling of them will help to keep their memory green."
J. I. Packer

Five Leading Reformers

Lives at a Watershed of History

Christopher Catherwood

Christopher Catherwood summarises the lives of Martin Luther, John Calvin, Ulrich Zwingli, Thomas Cranmer and John Knox. He unlocks the motivation, the power and drive that pushed these men to risk their position, their livelihoods and their lives.

ISBN: 978-1-84550-553-0

R.A. FINLAYSON

Reformed
Theological
Writings

"...penetrating and witty...
a gifted writer..."
CARL HENRY

Reformed Theological Writings
R. A. Finlayson

Prof R. A Finlayson was one of the most influential figures in the Free Church of Scotland in the twentieth century. As a preacher, conference speaker, editor of the monthly editor of the Monthly Record and as a professor of Systematic Theology at the Free Church college he exercised a fruitful ministry within and beyond his own denomination.

He wrote over a thousand articles, 32 of which are in this volume. They are divided into 3 sections: General Theology, Issues Facing Evangelicals and The Westminster Confession.

ISBN: 978-1-85792-259-2

CONTRIBUTORS
Rev. Terry L. Johnson • Dr. Robert S. Godfrey
Dr. Joseph A. Pipa, Jr. • Dr. Morton H. Smith
Rev. Brian Schwertley • Rev. Benjamin Shaw
Rev. Cliff Blair

The Worship of God

Reformed Concepts of Biblical Worship

The Worship of God
Reformed Concepts of Biblical Worship
Various

'There can be no more important issue than that of worship. There can be no more important question than that of how God is to be worshipped' In the 21st century, as has been the case throughout history, different interpretations of worship continue to divide churches and denominations. Worship expresses our theology and if we are to worship in truth we must submit to scriptural revelation. *The Worship of God* offers an invaluable companion to those seeking to enhance their understanding of the purpose, history and different forms of worship. Dealing with subject areas from the regulative principle of worship to the distinctives of reformed liturgy, from Heart worship to the place of Psalms and contemporary worship music, this book gives us unique insights on an issue that demands our attention.

ISBN: 978-1-84550-055-9

GRACE
ESSENTIALS

THE MINISTRY
WE NEED
THE REFORMED PASTOR

RICHARD BAXTER

The Ministry We Need

The Reformed Pastor

Richard Baxter

- Faithfully edited version of *The Reformed Pastor*
- For the modern reader
- For use by groups or individuals

Richard Baxter believed that teaching was the minister's main task. Equally, he believed that Christians should regularly approach their pastor with their problems, and that ministers should regularly disciple their congregations. Baxter's main concern was that personal instruction in the Bible should be given to everyone, not just the young. It was this concern that brought *The Reformed Pastor* to birth. Faithfully presented here in a version edited for the modern audience, this book offers helpful, practical advice for those in leadership positions.

ISBN: 978-1-5271-0103-6

Christian Focus Publications

Our mission statement —

STAYING FAITHFUL

In dependence upon God we seek to impact the world through literature faithful to His infallible Word, the Bible. Our aim is to ensure that the Lord Jesus Christ is presented as the only hope to obtain forgiveness of sin, live a useful life and look forward to heaven with Him.

Our books are published in four imprints:

CHRISTIAN
FOCUS

Popular works including biographies, commentaries, basic doctrine and Christian living.

CHRISTIAN
HERITAGE

Books representing some of the best material from the rich heritage of the church.

MENTOR

Books written at a level suitable for Bible College and seminary students, pastors, and other serious readers. The imprint includes commentaries, doctrinal studies, examination of current issues and church history.

CF4•K

Children's books for quality Bible teaching and for all age groups: Sunday school curriculum, puzzle and activity books; personal and family devotional titles, biographies and inspirational stories — because you are never too young to know Jesus!

Christian Focus Publications Ltd,
Geanies House, Fearn, Ross-shire,
IV20 1TW, Scotland, United Kingdom.
www.christianfocus.com
blog.christianfocus.com